"What happens when you break the heart of a young, black warlock from Harlem? Well, many frightening things."

- Jay Hunter

A DREADHEAD NAMED SAPPHIRE

The Second novel by

JAY HUNTER

Jay Hunter

ISBN: 9781541116566
ISBN-13: 1541116569

Dedication

I would like to dedicate this book to myself as it is very dear to my heart for many reasons. The African American Magician's series is a very large body of work that is deeply infused with times in my own personal life. This second novel reflects on some of those times but also of times that other people in my life have gone through. I can only hope that it will be accepted as a token of love to all my readers that support me in all that I create.

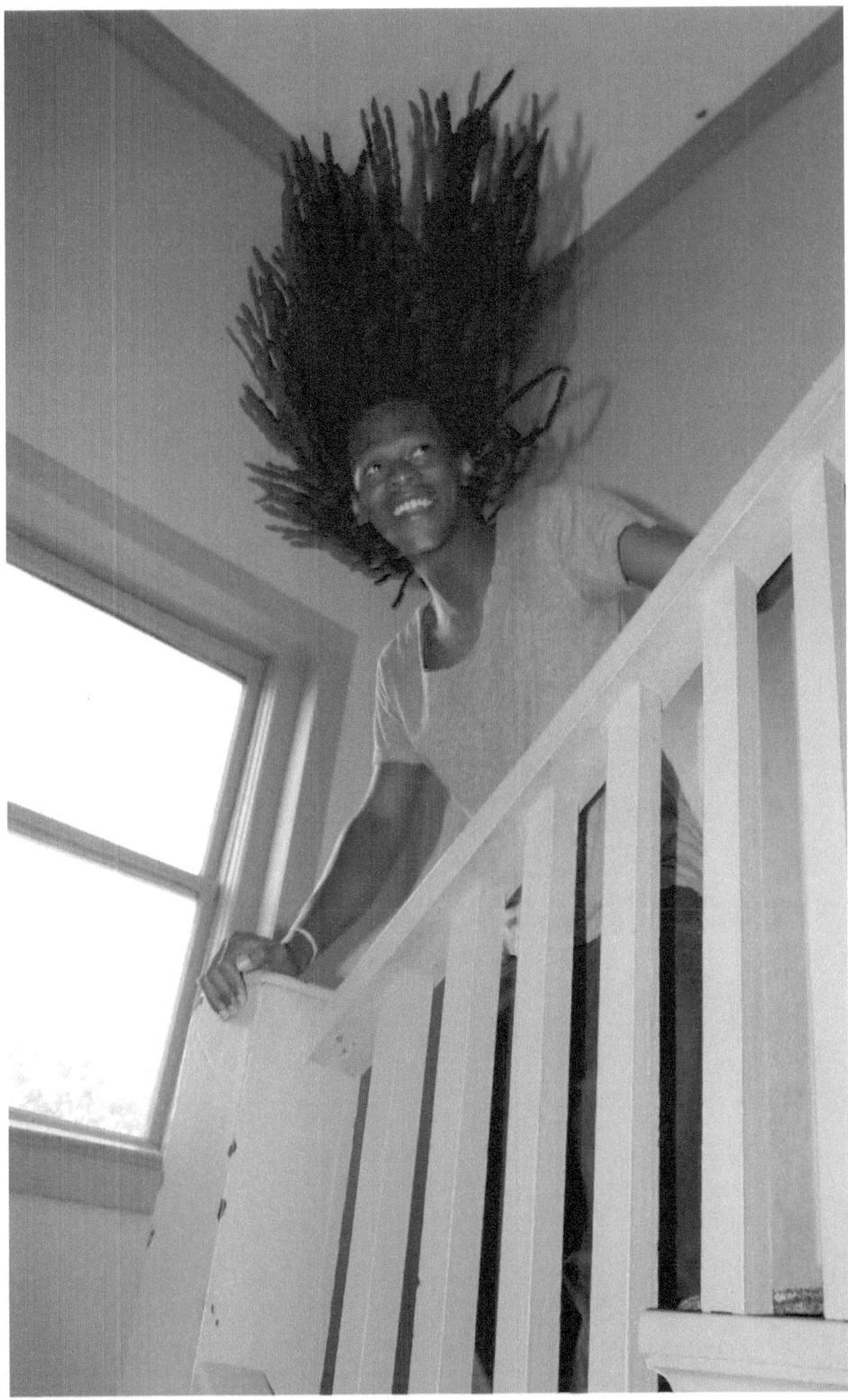

Jay Hunter

CONTENTS

A Dreadhead Named Sapphire

"Don't touch my hair."

- Jay

Jay Hunter

ACKNOWLEDGMENTS

I would like to acknowledge every African American artist that has paved the way for all of us that are of color to continue in the arts. All of the actors, musicians and creative forces that made it easier to believe that we could do anything if we worked hard and believed, I thank you.

I would also like to thank my parents, Chante Stevens and Jason Hunter Sr, for raising me up to believe I could achieve anything. I want to thank and give love to my grandparents for supporting and believing in my dreams.

To my friend, Moncherie Mac, thank you for artistic inspiration and moral support.

To my brothers and sister, for teaching me the importance of love, family, and brotherhood.

And I would like to thank my best friend Mr. Darius D. Snow for assistance of the interior and exterior design.

Jay Hunter

1 FAMILY

Sapphire Silas Bell awoke in his room, feeling the warmth of the autumn sun on his cheek. His dreadlocks strung across his face as he slowly got up to look over at his clock. It was 7:00 am in the morning, on November 28th, 1996, Thanks Giving day.

Sapphire was an African American poet and graduate from a Performing Art's high school in Harlem, where he lived. He was 5 feet tall, had brown skin, brown eyes and brown dreadlocks that stopped at his shoulders.

He lived with his mother named Marquette and his father named Leander, and he loved them very much. With no siblings, he stayed with them in a two-story townhouse on Graham Street.

He was cherished by his whole community and was well known for assisting the elderly and lending a hand to anyone that needed it.

His mother would often say that he had a sort of uniqueness that was not of this time, and his father would say that he was a young boy with an old soul.

Sapphire worked at a fitness gym, cleaning the weights and sweeping around for minimum wage. When he wasn't working, he would engulf himself in the arts, always writing his poetry, reading fantasy novels and watching documentaries and interviews on his favorite artists such as Jean Michel Basquiat and Maya Angelou.

He enjoyed music from the 1970's and would blast it on his boombox whenever he was cleaning up his room. He was happy and satisfied with the life he lived. He had his mother and father as his pillars and wouldn't even leave them for college like all his other classmates had done when graduating from high school two years back.

He had a girlfriend by the name of Seraphina. She was a beautiful, brown-skinned girl that he had met in high school. As an outcast in his classes, she was the only one to ever befriend him and they soon fell in love.

Sapphire cherished Seraphina, he always wrote poems about how much she meant to him. In high school, he would sneak into her dance class and watch her do ballet.

Seraphina had long, black hair that touched her back and the most beautiful hazel eyes; he would often wonder why she befriended him when she could have had any boy in school. He convinced himself that it was because she liked his artistic abilities and charm. But besides all that, there was something about him that she treasured, and that was his magic.

Sapphire was a natural, supernatural born warlock, which meant that he was a male magician. He had inherited his magic from his mother's line of the family that was rich in the magical Art's. His mother told him to be proud of the magic that he had but his father (that hadn't come from a line of magic) advised him to keep his uncanny gift a secret from people who couldn't do magic, and that seemed to be anyone outside of his mother's family.

Even though he kept his magic from the world, he didn't feel comfortable keeping it from his girlfriend. Sapphire had told Seraphina of his powers after a month of dating her. He had sworn not to keep secrets from her, and one night displayed his abilities in her room.

His act of revealing his secret represented the promise of their love; no secrets and no betrayal.

He levitated himself, changed the color of her gown and even summoned fire, all while speaking his spells that she thought sounded so romantic as they slid off his tongue. He had learned how to fluently use his magic to his will with the help of his spell book that his mom called a grimoire. He had learned how to control his magic from it after receiving it from his mother on the 25th of March when he had turned thirteen.

His grimoire was a manual of instructions on using his magic and even featured a few potions. The spell book had been passed down through four generations, dating back to Sapphire's great, great, grandfather who had purchased it from with a magic market in Shreveport.

Seraphina fainted in disbelief the first time that he had proved his powers to her, but after being around him so long she had gotten used to it. Together, they kept his magic a secret.

He stayed with his parents and she stayed with her grandmother just a bus ride away. She had turned 20 on the 25th of November and he had given her a promise ring that he had worked three months to pay for. He had told Seraphina that the ring represented their love going round and round and never-ending like an infinite circle. And he couldn't wait to see her after having dinner with his family.

On Thanksgiving, Sapphire would eat with his parents, his father's sister, Rene, and her three children. He couldn't wait to see them all.

Family was everything to Sapphire; he found strength in them all. He loved the click and clatter of pans and pots as everyone cooked and prepared his favorite dishes. He loved the gathering, the smiles and the outburst of laughter from one of his father's many jokes.

After he would spend time with his family, he'd go see Seraphina and take her to a movie. They planned to go out at night, after stuffing their coats full of snacks to go see a film called Set It Off.

Bringing snack stuffed coats to the movies was a big tradition that they both loved to partake in. Seraphina would sneak a bite of Sapphire's food after eating hers and he would sneak a kiss in between scenes. After the movie was over, the two would throw popcorn at the screen if they didn't like it and then run out to avoid being caught.

After showering, Sapphire walked out of his bathroom in a brown turtleneck and tan slacks that he had found under a pile of clothes on the floor. His room was often a wreck; he was a gentleman but a very messy one. He barely kept his possessions tidy and to his father's disgust, would come in and drop his clothes on the floor after getting undressed.

Sapphire walked down his steps with his socks sliding against the wooden steps. He had dressed up, but he wasn't putting on shoes - that was too much.

"Hey, mom," he said as he walked into the kitchen where his mother was snapping collard greens in the sink.

Marquette was the same height as he was. She wore a chocolate brown sweater and her hair was in one of her usual ponytails.

"Hey, baby," said Marquette, her almond eyes on Sapphire as he opened the oven to spy on the turkey. "It's about time you came down here; I need you to stir that dressing on the stove, boy."

"Okay," Sapphire said.

"And, I want you to use your hands to do it. I keep telling you to stop using your magic to do everything, that's lazy. I saw that mop down here cleaning the floor by itself last night. Magic is a very serious thing; if you use it to fix all your problems in life it might backfire on you one day. I use my magic to heal, it shouldn't be used selfishly."

"Sorry, mom," said Sapphire. He stirred the dressing on the stove with a silver spoon as he heard his mother go on about how he should use magic, rolling his eyes when she wouldn't stop.

"And don't be showing off in front of your cousins like you did last year. Your aunt had to threaten them not to go to school and tell their friends about their big cousin that can turn a spoon into a LIT CANDLE."

"Okay, okay, Mom, I understand. Now, will you please stop talking to me like I'm five?"

"Watch your tone with me," Marquette said, her finger in Sapphire's face, laughing as he pretended to bite it. "You look really nice, I like that turtleneck."

"Thank you, mom," said Sapphire. "And where's dad?"

"He's on his way home, I sent him out to get juice,"

"Oh, okay"

"Do me a favor and add some milk to that macaroni, and with your hands."

"Okay," Sapphire groaned, he hated cooking but loved eating afterward. He had a very big appetite but was as skinny as a toothpick. He poured the milk into the macaroni and then ran to answer the phone from the living room. "Hello," he said.

"Hey, Blue," said a very familiar voice.

Sapphire knew who was calling. His grandparents that he called Mema and Pepa were calling from Buck Range Arkansas, where they lived. His grandmother would call him blue because when he was born the whites of his eyes were a sapphire blue for a full day, granting him his name.

Sapphire's parents were both from Buck Range and had moved to New York as a young couple for a more fast paste life, and to escape their overbearing parents. On Christmas, Sapphire's grandparents would come down to visit him and he would love to be in their loving arms after not seeing them for so long. "Howdy," said Sapphire, a large smile across his face.

"How's my favorite grandson doing on this fine, glorious Thanks Giving day?"

"I'm doing great," Sapphire snickered. He always thought it was funny to be called Mema's favorite grandson because he was her only grandson.

"Are you still working at that fitness gym, training folks? Your Pepa said are you trying to be a bodybuilder?" Mema asked.

"No, Mema, I only clean at the gym. I don't train people." Sapphire slapped his head with his hand.

"Oh," said Mema. "Well, how's Seraphina doing,

y'all still together?"

"Yes Ma'am, we are."

"Your Pepa said when are y'all getting married."

Sapphire smiled, "When she gets down on one knee and pops the question."

"Wow," Mema chuckled. "Well, I'm glad you guys are still together How are you handling your anger problem?"

Sapphire placed his hand over his head. He didn't want to talk about that right now. He didn't like to think about his condition much.

He didn't want to ever discuss his diagnosis. Two years back, in high school, he had been diagnosed with Intermittent Explosive Disorder, after coming home and destroying his room out of anger. He had been bullied very badly by a boy named Cerberus who was in the same grade as he was.

Sapphire had told his parents that he had had enough and needed to take his aggression out on something. He thought it wasn't such a problem but his parents feared that his anger issues would grow after he continued to outburst when pushed too far.

He was a good person who didn't want to hurt anyone, but when he was angry he would lose his will to care what was around. An object thrown, a loud scream or shaking was usual when he was upset.

He was prescribed medication that his father's money could afford but he didn't take them. He simply would refuse his medication and say, "I'm not crazy, only crazy people need those."

"I've been doing okay, I haven't had an outburst in three weeks, Mema," Sapphire whispered.

"Well, that's great, Blue," Mema said. "Remember what I told you before when you feel like people are pulling you past your limits you need to remove yourself from them. And don't let nobody control you. Don't be a trash can for nobody, no one should dump their negativity in you. And keep writing that poetry, art is a great way to let out your aggression."

"Yes ma'am," Sapphire said as he noticed his mother approaching him. "Let me talk to Mama, said Marquette, "I need you to go watch those mashed potatoes for me."

"Got to go, Mema, love you guys,"

"We love you too, Blue. And when I come back down for your next birthday I'm gonna beat you in go-carts, again," Mema said.

She wasn't the average grandmother who sat in a rocking chair and knitted. At the age of 56 she loved loud music, go-carts and slapping her bass whenever she felt in the mood. She was the best.

Sapphire chuckled as he handed the phone to his mother and walked back into the kitchen.

"Hey, big man," said Leander, as he came in through the back door with a grocery sack in his hand.

Sapphire had gotten his eyes, height and cheekbones from his mother but had inherited his father's nose, allergies, and his loud laugh. Leander didn't have dreadlocks like Sapphire's, instead, he kept his hair faded and always tried to convince Sapphire to get one as well; but Sapphire always declined because he loved his dreadlocks; always calling them his crown.

"Hey, daddy," Sapphire said as he dapped his father up. "You've got to save me; mom's got me in here on kitchen duty."

"What, Marquette, you've got this boy in here

doing your dirty work?"

"One minute," said Marquette, "I'm on the phone with, mama."

"Dad, can I have twenty dollar's?" Sapphire asked as he watched his father's face turn sour.

"What?" asked Leander as he took his black jacket off and hung it on the coat rack by the basement door. "Don't you got a job, son?"

"Yeah, dad, but I don't get paid until next Friday. I'm taking Seraphina out and I need some dough, come on dad, please, I'll pay you back. I tried to summon some money the other day and nearly had a seizure."

"That's cause you ain't supposed to do that. Your mom said that stuff is very powerful and dangerous; it's not to be played with. We work for our money in this family."

"Okay, okay, you're right."

"Here," said Leander, handing Sapphire a twenty dollar bill from his leather wallet.

"Thanks, Dad!" Sapphire said as he smiled.

Marquette had gotten off the phone and came back into the kitchen to see what the two were up to.

"You ain't watching them potatoes, boy!" she said.

"Got to go," Sapphire said as he rushed past his mother and ran upstairs to his room. He dialed Seraphina's number and waited patiently for her to answer.

"Hello," she said, her voice light, almost in a whisper.

"Hey, girl, Happy Thanksgiving" Sapphire said, a large smile across his face.

He hadn't seen Seraphina in a day and that was too long for him. He had to hear her voice.

"Hey, baby, happy Thanksgiving to you too," said Seraphina. "I was just thinking of you when I heard our song on the radio. You know, the one by Tony Terry."

"Oh, When I'm With You?"

"That's it."

"Sing it to me," Sapphire said, "Refresh my memory."

Seraphina had a very pretty voice besides being able to dance, and Sapphire loved to hear it.

"No, Sapphire, I don't want to sing, it's too early. I sound like a frog."

"Well, you'll just have to sing it to me tonight, love, when we go see Set It Off."

"Okay," Seraphina said. "I really can't wait."

Sapphire giggled, "Me neither."

"Oh, how's your grandma doing, is she still having those bad chest pains?"

"Yeah, and she's tryna' get out of cooking today, so, it looks like you're gonna have to bring some Thanksgiving dinner with you to the movies."

"Really?"

"Yeah, I'm gonna go check on her, just meet me at my house at 7:00 pm and we'll catch the bus from there."

"Okay, tell her I said hi."

"Aight."

"Love you," Sapphire said. He could never get off the phone with his family without telling them that he loved them. It wasn't a superstitious thing but a moral value. If this was his last word with his loved one it was going to be something meaningful.

"Love you, bye" Seraphina said as she hung up her phone.

Usually, Seraphina wouldn't be so quick over the phone but he didn't really ponder on why she got off so fast. He got up to go get some candy that he had stashed in his drawer and heard the front door downstairs open. He knew that that couldn't have been anyone else but his Aunt Rene. She was here with his three cousins and he tossed his candy on his bed and rushed down his steps to see them.

His aunt Rene, his father's sister, stood at the door talking to Marquette as her three children stood around her. Rene had very bright skin and a round face that was covered by her dark brown curly hair. Her three children were named Rose, the eldest, Timothy and Angel, and they were all very close in age to Sapphire.

While Rene, Leander and Marquette finished preparing the food in the kitchen, Sapphire and his cousins watched cartoons on the television while debating over topics such as TLC being better than Xscape and Dexter's Laboratory being funnier than The Rugrats. After the debate had been ended by Marquette announcing that it was time to eat, the four settled at the dinner table in the kitchen and each said what they were thankful for.

Yams, greens, stuffing, brisket and a piping hot turkey sat on a well decorated table. Biscuits were buttered, pies were pulled out of the oven and the smell of Sapphires favorite baked beans, from his father's hands, sat right in front of him. Everyone passed plates downward until there was nothing left to pass.

Sapphire smirked because he thought it was funny that the blue plates they were about to use were only allowed twice a year for Christmas and Thanksgiving.

His mother was strict with her dinnerware, because Sapphire would clumsily drop them. He would be doomed to eat from paper plates after tonight.

After everyone had said what they were thankful for, it was now Sapphire's turn. He pulled out a piece of wrinkled paper from his back pocket and stood up in front of everyone, a smile on his face. He was about to read a poem that he wrote titled: When I'm With Family.

"I wrote a poem," he said. "And I wanted to read it to everyone. It's about what I'm truly thankful for."

"Oh, beautiful," Rene said, with proud eye's.

"Alright, here it goes," Sapphire said, with a slight clearing of his throat.

And he read:

"When I feel lost and all my joy is gone, I turn to my family and they help me to hold on."

"That's a good start, there, boy," his father said, making everyone giggle.

"Shush, and listen to my baby," said his mother.

"When my head hurts and my life has gone wrong I lean on them, because they're all so strong. They greet me with loving arms stretched out long. When I am with family I am truly home.

"They give me knowledge for food and food for the soul. They give me insight on how to tackle my goals. They teach me lessons that I'll need when on my own.

"When I am with family I am truly whole. In this life, it can get crappy. I've cried many tears that made my throat feel raspy. But when I laugh with my mother or joke with my daddy. I realize that when I'm with family I am truly happy."

There was an unexpectedly loud applause from

everyone around. The joy on their faces made Sapphire feel a warm glow in his heart.

"That was beautiful, neph," said Rene.

Rose turned and looked over at Marquette. "This boy is good," she said. "It was short but it was great. I need to hear more of your stuff."

His older cousin, Rose, was always so supportive of him, after all, she had been the one who had inspired him to start writing, after he had read some of her poetry as a teenager.

"Thanks, y'all," Sapphire said. He smiled, largely, as if he had won a prize and was being honored for it. "Now let's eat!" he said as he sat at the foot of the table, towards his father who sat at the head.

"That's what I'm saying," Leander said as he began to carve the turkey and serve it to everyone. "I need to get enough in my system so I can beat Rene in some dominoes!"

"Whatever, Leander," Rene said. "You gone lose like you did last time."

Topics, such as how long Sapphire's hair had grown since last year and how tall Timothy had gotten, made everyone chatty, and once they were talking about a black boy they moved on to a black boy getting shot by a cop. Sapphire hated to hear about injustice in his community. The police were shooting unarmed black people more and more each month. He felt as if his own African American population was being downsized by the people that were supposed to protect it. It hurt.

"You know that one boy got shot last week? What's his name – oh, Chauncey, he was shot right on his mama's porch," said Rene.

"Really?" Marquette asked. "That's a shame. What

was their excuse this time?"

"The cop said that he thought the boy was pulling a gun out to shoot them when they were arresting someone across the street," Rene said. "His Mama said that he was only pulling out a comb!"

"Idiots!" said Leander.

"They stay trying to put us underground," said Rose, rolling her eyes.

"I'm just worried about my boy going out in a world where cops want to destroy our black men," said Rene.

"Me too," Marquette added, looking over at Sapphire. "Me too."

Sapphire took a sip of his grape juice. "It don't make no sense. And I heard the cop got paid leave."

"Yea," said Leander. "They gave 'em a vacation for killing a brotha'."

"Right," Sapphire said.

"We matter in this community and somebody is going to show them that one day," said Marquette. "I ain't saying every cop is racist, but, the 60s aren't so far away from us. It used to be okay to hang us 30 years ago. Some of those old and hateful cops' children are on the force now."

"Sho' right?" said Sapphire.

"Hey, can Sapphire do some of his magic for us," said Timothy. "All this talk about cops is boring me."

"No," said Rene, "I told you not to ask, that when we got here, boy. We talked about this in the car."

"We don't want Sapphire turned into no circus attraction," said Leander. "Plus we want him to use his gift wisely. Ain't that right, son?"

"Right, dad," Sapphire said before he looked over at Timothy and winked. He knew immediately that

that meant he would do something magical when everyone had had dessert and left them alone to go watch football. Sapphire never was interested in sports, it bored him. He'd rather read a book, write, or paint.

There was a small, one level, concrete building that he painted in when he felt overwhelmed with life. It was next to a closed high way and Sapphire had been given the keys to it from his father's friend, who had used it as a headquarters for his bus company before.

His name was Mr. White and he knew how much Sapphire loved to paint. He had moved out of the space a year ago and had given it to Sapphire for a therapeutic, resting place once he had heard of his anger issues (Leander wasn't good at keeping things to himself and Sapphire hated that).

He would even practice monologues that he wrote himself. He had done theater in high school and loved it. The joy of becoming another character or walking in someone else's shoes was such a brilliant experience for him, at least that's what he'd always say.

Seraphina had been to the building twice, but wouldn't go anymore after admitting how creepy she thought it was. Sapphire wasn't afraid to be in it by himself, it was just four concrete walls with two large windows and a place where he could be all of him.

2 LOVE

After chatting about poetry with Rose, wrestling with Timothy and showing Angel that he could make his spoon bend by his magic, Sapphire was ready to go see Seraphina.

He waved everyone good bye, knowing that his cousin's would be gone by the time he came back. He took a short bus ride to see Seraphina at her home and was now on her front porch.

After a few knocks, Seraphina opened the door wearing her long hair down her back. She wore a red halter top with baggy, blue jeans and a burgundy over coat that hung off her shoulders. Her wheat colored boots were laced very lazy like, and her tube socks were ruffled down.

Sapphire really liked how her style could change. She could dress like a Tom Boy one day and the President's daughter the next.

"Hey, babe," she said as she gave Sapphire a peck on his lips.

"Ready?" asked Sapphire.

"Yup."

"You look gorgeous, baby."

"Thank you."

"Who is that, sweet heart?" asked a faint voice from down the hall.

"It's Sapphire, grandma," said Seraphina. "Go on back to sleep."

"Tell em I said hi."

"I will, grandma, now gone and get some rest."

"What y'all bout to do, child?"

"Grandma," said Seraphina as Sapphire snickered. It wasn't freezing cold but he wanted to be on the warm bus, instead of standing outside her door.

He wanted to drive his father's car to get her, but, unlike the money, Leander wasn't giving that up easily. He would barely let Sapphire's mother drive it.

"Bye, grandma, we're gone," said Seraphina, rolling her eyes as she closed her front door. "I had to get out of this house, Sapphire. I'm so glad we could go out tonight."

"Me too," said Sapphire, as he reached in his leather coat pocket to hand Seraphina a rose that he had enchanted to glow from pink to bright red. "For you."

"Awe, thank you, babe," Seraphina said as she and Sapphire began to stroll down the street to catch their bus. "It's beautiful."

"Not more beautiful than you," said Sapphire.

Seraphina grabbed a hold of his hands. "You know I'm really the luckiest girl in the world. I'm so glad I've got you —"

Sapphire gave Seraphina a kiss that stopped her from finishing her sentence. He loved to hear her talk but feeling her lips against his was an even greater experience.

"I'm the lucky one," he said. "Cause I've got you."

Love was a very serious thing to Sapphire; he had been brought up with it as his family's foundation. To him, family represented everything love was about. Patience, kindness, giving, whole hearted feelings; these were all things he said a family couldn't survive

17

without. These were all the things he said love stood for.

Sapphire had stopped Seraphina to spin her by her delicate wrist in the park that they had first made their love official. They were on a long slab of concrete that had statues of baby cupids around it.

Sapphire would always make sure they walked through this area when on a date. It meant a lot to him, the architecture, the sculpture design, the memories.

They were dropped off a block from the theater and they walked down a busy street, holding hands, as the night wind brushed against their faces.

People were shopping around the plaza hustling and racing to their cars for warmth. Shoppers were walking around looking into department store windows and Sapphire stopped Seraphina to show her a necklace in the view.

He smiled before saying, "I'm gone get you that, girl, one day. I promise."

"Really?" said Seraphina as she took his hands again.

"Of course. I'll get you whatever you want when I get a real job, or finally start getting paid for my work, like Basquiat used to. "I know you are worth more than jewelry but it still looks good on you."

Seraphina didn't speak. She just looked down. Then she said, "you really think that I'm worth more. I'm not perfect, I don't even think I deserve you, Sapphire – "

"No, no, no, don't say that. You're my girl and I don't care what you've done in the past, I think you are everything. Now fix ya' face, so we can go see this movie." Sapphire snickered as he caressed the side of

Seraphina's face, "I love you, girl."

Not even a popcorn crumb was thrown at the screen after the amazing performance from the four African American actresses in Set It Off. Sapphire nearly cried a few times but was sure that Seraphina had. To him, the film represented the struggles of the black community: poverty, loss, greed and unraveling emotions.

It was beautiful, it was sad, it was ghetto', it was magnificent.

The two had eaten all their snacks in the movie theater but were still hungry. They ate donuts at a 24 hour coffee shop with exposed brick and wooden floors.

"You know," said Seraphina, "I cried so much in that movie. It just had a deep...I don't know...it was just...."

"Too much," said Sapphire.

"Yeah," said Seraphina. "Too much. It's just so sad."

Usually after a movie the two would be joking all the way home and roasting each other; but tonight they were quiet, as still as the unbothered coffee in their mugs on the table. The film had them all shook up.

"I've been thinking of moving out one day," Sapphire said, in hopes of ending the silence between him and Seraphina. "I can't stay with my parents forever and I just feel like I need a place of my own. And you could come live with me...I know you get tired of being with your grandma sometimes."

"Yeah, that'd be great. We would be kicking it."

"You bet. Man, I really wanted to read this poem to you but I left it at the building."

"What was it about?" Seraphina asked, looking deprived.

"Nah, I think I'll keep it a secret until I get it. I don't want you burning over just the title. I want you to digest the whole thing, baby."

"Aw, whatever, Sapphire. You know I love your poetry. Art...is such a beautiful thing."

"You right on that, baby."

She shared the same views as he did and he loved that. Sapphire loved how much the two had in common. They both enjoyed film, art, pop culture, music and good, deep conversations. He could talk to her forever about the galaxy or a new brand of chips, both subjects would last for at least two hours.

Sapphire looked over at a chalk bored with a special that was scratched over with a white chalk line. He chuckled.

"What's so funny?" asked Seraphina.

Sapphire looked at her and smiled "Nothing, I just...I just was looking at the chalk board...menu over there." He pointed to the right, over Seraphina's shoulder. "It reminds me of Basqiuat."

"How does a chalk board remind you of Basqiuat?"

"Well, I read that he crossed out word's in his works of art that he wanted people to pay attention to more...one of the items on the menu is crossed out. I just think that's so cool. It's so fresh, the things that are in Basqiuat's mind, you'd think that he was scratching out words so you wouldn't see them...but he's doing that to draw you in closer to them. The guys a genius."

"You just love Basqiuat, don't you?"

"Of course," said Sapphire. "Really, I do. But not more than you, never. I love you, girl."

Seraphina stretched over the table to kiss Sapphire on his lips. "I love you too, Sapphire," she said.

3 INFORMATION

Two days had gone past since the late night date with Seraphina. Sapphire was upstairs in his room cleaning up for the first time in a week. He swept and picked up all his clothes (manually) while wearing a white T and sweats.

He was listening to some jazz on his boom box while doing an uncoordinated dance that he had seen a Spanish man do on an old television show. He was horrible at dancing.

While finishing up his room he heard his mother and father downstairs yelling. It sounded as if they were in the living room. He hated when his parents would argue. The sounds of hollering, the spits and spats, it made him sick.

He stood in the middle of the steps to eavesdrop and heard his mother say that she was getting a divorce.

Sapphire didn't move. Or breathe. He felt his heart turn to ice and maybe even shatter a little. That was the last word he wanted to hear and yet his mother said it three more times over his father's begging.

What had happened?

His parents had been in situations before, but they had always recovered. They had always bounced back. Now they were splitting up.

"You thought I wasn't gone find out you were cheating on me?" Marquette asked, her voice full of grief. She sounded as if she was about to cry, Sapphire hated to hear his mother cry.

"I'm sorry, baby," Leander said, his voice full of frustration, "you know she didn't mean nothing!"

Sapphire didn't want to believe that his father had done what he was accused of but he knew. He knew and he was angry. All of the late nights, and the many excuses that followed after.

It had now been revealed. Leander was a cheater. Sapphire's mother stayed home keeping it and loving her family. She dedicated her life to her son and her husband but Leander was giving his appreciation away to another woman. This was vial, this was sick.

"It's over!" said Marquette as Leander began to cry. "It's over."

Those word's shook Sapphire's mind and rattled his spine. His family was going to be split, right down the middle. He would be a son of a broken home. It was over, everything was over. His parents had been married for the twenty years that he lived on this earth and now he would have to live the rest of his life without them together.

And it was all his father's fault. Sapphire ran to his room and pulled a wooden hammer from out of his utility supplies. He ran downstairs without any shoes, past his parents, through the front door and headed for his dad's green, 1976 Mustang.

"Sapphire, what are you doing?" asked Marquette as Leander ran outside after him.

Sapphire climbed atop his father's car, and with all his might, busted the front window to pieces.

"Stop!" Leander yelled as he looked up at

Sapphire who was standing on the hood, his hammer deeply gripped by his sweaty palm.

"You stupid idiot!" Sapphire said, looking down at his father. "All she ever did was love you! All she ever did was give you every piece of her, every inch and every ounce and you cheated on her!?"

"Sapphire, get down!" Leander and Marquette yelled as Sapphire continued to damage the Mustang, his eyes dripping with tears, his throat burning.

"Don't touch him, Leander," Marquette yelled. "You know he's not thinking clearly. He has a condition, Leander, you know that."

"What am I supposed to do!?" Leander asked as he looked over at Marquette and back at Sapphire, his eyes full of confusion.

Sapphire stopped smashing his father's car but it wasn't because he kept begging him to, but, the neighborhood was coming out of their homes, everyone was watching him. The sweet, respectful Sapphire that they knew now looked like a dangerous hoodlum. He felt so embarrassed.

"You ain't been taking your medication," said Leander, looking at Sapphire as if he was an animal that needed to be caged.

Sapphire pointed his hammer at his father, "I told you I'm not crazy. Only crazy people take those."

"Come down, baby," said Marquette. "Please."

Sapphire jumped down from his father's car, butted past him and ran upstairs to his room.

"Where are you going, don't you think you owe me an apology?" Leander asked as he and Marquette walked back into the house behind their son.

Marquette stopped Leander by the steps as Sapphire stomped up to his room. "Don't hurt my boy, Leander."

As Sapphire waved his hand around his room, all his clothes flew into a suitcase that had sprung onto his bed. He put on his white Chucks and packed his toothbrush, locking jell, lotion and deodorant. Leander and Marquette came into his room both trying to convince him to just sit down and stop packing.

"I'm leaving," Sapphire said. "I can't stay under the roof of a no good, dirtbag!"

"Sapphire, please stay," said Marquette.

"Yeah, boy, don't leave, I'll go," Leander yelled as he touched Sapphire's shoulder.

"GET OFF!" Sapphire screamed as his father's body rose up and slammed into the wall.

"You have to control your magic," Marquette said, standing back by Sapphire's closet as Leander stuck to the wall, his gray hoodie looking as if it was made of a strong adhesive.

Both his parents looked at him as he realized within himself that he didn't know he could levitate past his own body weight. He was getting stronger. More at ease with his abilities.

"I've got to go, Mama," Sapphire said as he threw on his black leather jacket. "I love you, dearly, but I've got to get the heck away from this punk."

"Please, don't go," Marquette asked as Sapphire exited his room, Leander's body falling to the floor as he went downstairs.

His mother ran after him as his father held onto his shoulder that was starting to ache.

Sapphire hugged his mother very tightly, her tears smashing against his cheek.

Marquette put her hands together. "Why won't

you just stay?"

"Mama, please don't cry I can't see you crying like this…. I'm just going to go stay with Seraphina. I just can't stay here; I don't want to see him ever again. I need some time away. This is his house and I won't live off that rat no more. Mama, I'm out, love you."

And after that, Sapphire left his parents' home and headed down the street to catch the bus. He had to hide his tears from everyone who stood out on their porch. In Harlem, the neighbors were very nosey, everyone wanted the scoop, everyone seemed to be bloodthirsty for information.

Their eyes were like cameras, their expressions like heat lamps on a summer day. He felt them judging him, he felt them thinking that he was a nut job; he hated to be viewed in that way.

The yellow leaves above his head, in the trees on the sidewalk, were the only thing that kept him from focusing on everyone's stares. They fell over him as if adorning him as if showering him with blessings, he thought it was beautiful.

Fall was his second favorite season, besides spring. It felt like a mother's love, warm yet easy to love, not unforgiving and bitter like winter was.

On the bus ride to Seraphina's, Sapphire looked straight, barely blinking and barely turning his head to look out of his window. He felt broken inside, like his father had damaged something in him that he needed to make his body function, perhaps his heart?

Cheating was a low and dirty thing to Sapphire. He didn't understand how someone could say that they loved another, commit to them and then break their vow and give their passion to another, who wasn't even worthy of it.

And who was this woman, Sapphire thought. Was she white, or black? Was she skinnier than his mother, younger, maybe?

He couldn't believe this. Thanksgiving was just two days ago and everything seemed okay. The laughter, the joy, the love. Everything was fine. What else could any other woman offer his father? What else could be better than his beautiful mother?

4 REVELATION

Sapphire sat in Seraphina's room that was full of bronze, burgundy and orange colors. Like his mother, she hated pink, nothing was really girly in her room, instead, it had a grown woman vibe to itself. He sat on her bed to tell her everything that had just happened as she went through her clothes in her closet.

"Man, at least you got to know your parents," she said as she laid out some clothes next to Sapphire. "I mean, I feel for you, baby, but I ain't even seen my parents hold hands, or hold my hands for that matter. You don't seem too calm, did you bring your medication?"

"I ain't took that medication in I don't know how long, Seraphina. I don't bother with it."

"Well, I'm not gone pressure you to take it but I want you to stay here like you said you was, don't go back to that house or something terrible might happen."

"Okay," Sapphire said as he looked over at Seraphina. "You are so beautiful, girl."

Seraphina chuckled, her body now sprawled out on her bed, beside Sapphire. "Thank you."

"Why are those clothes out, you going somewhere?"

"I wanted to go to this house party that my homegirl invited me to, but I probably won't go now. I'ma' stay here with you, baby."

"No, no, go have fun," said Sapphire as Seraphina toyed with his dreadlocks. "We can chill here and watch some movies until it's time for you to go, and then I'll probably just go to sleep while you out. Don't let me spoil the fun."

"Okay," Seraphina said, "but if my grandma knock on this door while I'm gone don't answer it. She's kinda' lost her mind."

"No I haven't," said Seraphina's grandmother, her voice coming through the cracks in her door.

"Grandma, get away from my door! How long have you been there?"

"Long enough to know I'm getting a raise," said Seraphina's grandmother.

Sapphire chuckled as Seraphina rushed out her room to give her grandmother a good talking to. They cheered him up. They took his mind off of issues, at least for a little while.

After a roasting battle, cartoons and fits of random laughter it was 9:30pm and Seraphina was heading out in a red leather jacket and baggy jeans. Sapphire was flipping through the pages of his grimoire as she sprayed perfume on her neck and then gave him a gentle kiss goodbye.

"Don't come back with no baby," Sapphire joked as Seraphina cackled while leaving out of her room.

"Love you," he yelled.

"Love you too," said Seraphina's grandmother from her room down the hall, and that made him burst into a fit of laughter. Being over Seraphina's was the medicine he needed.

He slept for a little while, after over thinking everything like he always did.

When I'm With You was playing on the radio, on

29

Seraphina's dresser, softly. She wasn't here to sing it with him and as he rested on her bed, spread eagle, he noticed that he was missing her. It was now 10:30 and he wanted to see her. Feelings of anger towards his father had begun to spring up in him again and he needed her to tell him another joke to make him forget it all. He tried writing a poem but snatched the paper right out of its binding, fighting the air after it landed on the ground.

He was so upset. Looking at himself in the round vanity mirror in front of him with his hands through his hair and his eyes watering made him feel embarrassed. He had to gain self-control. He had to see Seraphina. He had to be happy again.

He couldn't concentrate on his poetry; too much was circulating his mind like: where his father was now, and why his mother hadn't called to check on him yet. Was she upset with him?

After using a locator spell to find her, Sapphire came up to a red house that was at least three stories tall. He knew Seraphina would be here, the loud music and people outside convinced him that he was indeed at a house party. But this house, it was familiar. He had seen it before. Sapphire had been by this house every day when he was in high school, his bus driver had a let-off stop here. Cerberus lived here, and after verbally abusing Sapphire every day he would jump off the bus and go into this very house.

The memories of the bully who had tortured Sapphire at his school all flooded him. Cerberus was a tall, dark and mean young boy who was a star athlete and a popular jug head in high school. His hobbies included winning every trophy he could, bringing his school fame, having multiple girlfriends and hurting

Sapphire as best he could.

Sapphire had been thrown in a trash can, locked in a locker and pushed by Cerberus at least twice a week, every week. Sapphire hated him.

He was no good to him.

All Cerberus was really good at was bouncing a ball and the school they attended had made a trophy room at the end of the first-floor hall with all of his memorabilia and pictures of his success. They called him a hero, the staff did because he could shoot a free throw; but to Sapphire, he was nothing but a horrible excuse for a young man with no regard for any living thing but himself.

The house looked exactly the same as it did two years back, except for a gutter that was fixed. Sapphire had a great memory; he could even remember the white color that the mailbox in front was before it was painted red.

Why was Seraphina here? She knew how much he hated Cerberus. She knew he wouldn't like her at his house party. He walked towards the house and saw a young, black boy with French braids and a wife beater on. He stood with a 40 ounce in his hand and he was talking to a young girl with long, red weave, they were by the front door.

"Hey, Sapphire," said the girl with red weave.

Sapphire recognized who she was, her name was Ell and the guy next to her was her boyfriend, Augustus. They had dated in high school and were still going strong.

"What you here for, square?" said Augustus, a shy smile across his face.

He was one of the many people that copied off of Sapphire's work in class so he wasn't ever a bully to him. He was a thug, but Sapphire wasn't intimidated or moved at the slightest. He didn't view thugs and gang bangers in the same manner as everyone else did in New York. He saw past their hard exteriors and looked at the child-like innocents in them. They were never more or less than that unless they tried to hurt him but that never happened. The only one that enjoyed causing him pain was Cerberus and he knew he was about to see him as he paced closer to his front door.

"I'm here to see my girl, Seraphina," said Sapphire as Augustus wiped his mouth.

"You don't wanna do that, buddy," he said. "Just go home."

"What?" Sapphire said as he looked at Augustus.

"You don't wanna go in there, brotha'," Augustus sounded so drunk, that's one thing Sapphire didn't like, drunkenness.

"I'm just here to see my girl, Cerberus ain't gone stop me from doing that," Sapphire said.

"Yo' girl is in there all on dude," Augustus yelled.

Sapphire's eyes were locked in on Augustus. He couldn't get a word out but his mouth was wide open.

"Mmmhmm, now look at cha'," Augustus said as Ell looked down at her feet. "You couldn't just go home, huh? Seraphina in there with her lips all on Cerberus, dog, she all over 'em."

"My girl, my girl would never be all on any dude," Sapphire said.

"You sure bout dat —"

"Positive, Augustus."

"Aight, well, go on in, man. Have a look fo' ya' self."

Sapphire slowly pushed past Augustus and

opened the white door to Cerberus' house. His stomach was twisted in knots and his teeth were chattering, he didn't know what he was about to see. As if time wasn't on his side, he had come in just to get a view of Seraphina in the arms of a tall, dark man. Cerberus was indeed holding his lover, his friend, his future wife.

This could not be.

She looked happy as everyone around danced to slow jams; she looked pleased to be in his company, in his home and in his arms.

"What are you doing?" Sapphire asked. "What are…what's going on here, Seraphina?"

In an instant, Seraphina pushed Cerberus away, his face scrunched up as he smoothed out his box haircut. She looked startled.

"Sapphire…y–y said…you was gone stay home," Seraphina said, seeing the tears well up in Sapphire's eyes. "Why…did you come, why did you…?"

Sapphire looked at Seraphina and then at Cerberus.

"Get lost, faggot," Cerberus said as he put his arms back around Seraphina, to Sapphire's surprise she didn't fight him off, she just looked at him.

"Why…Seraphina…why?" Sapphire felt a tidal wave of emotions rush through him. He felt alone, he felt hurt, he felt angry.

He was being cheated on just like his mother. She had gotten betrayed by her husband and now he was being hurt by the love of his life. It was as if his world had ended. Seraphina's cold eyes didn't show any sympathy, she looked a little interrupted, but not sorry at all.

Someone had once said in school that nice guys

finished last and he wondered if that was a prophecy for his own life.

His world was crashing before his very eyes.

"Get outta' here, faggot," Cerberus said, again, as if Sapphire needed another example that he thought nothing of him. "Me and ya' girl been sneakin' and creepin' for a whole three months, it's about time yo' dumb butt found out, busta'."

Seraphina just looked lost now, all she said was, "sorry, Sapphire."

Her word's meant nothing. Her actions spoke louder. Sapphire was done. He backed away from the two, slowly, his eyes dripping with tears.

"Aye, get outta here with all that crying stuff, man," Cerberus said as Sapphire continued to back away.

After high school, Sapphire thought he'd be free from the pestilent Cerberus but Seraphina had drug him back into the picture. He had to come for his girl, he couldn't just be satisfied with the many girls he already had.

Sapphire left the house in a steady speed, not to fast not too slow, with tears falling to the concrete. He wasn't going back to Seraphina's home. In his black backpack that he wore was his spell book, pen and writing journal. He could get another toothbrush but couldn't find a grimoire as special as the one he owned; and his writing journal was full of written poems.

He was on his way to the concrete building under the abandoned highway.

When he arrived at his fortress, he walked in and turned on the lights. His father's friend was even nice enough to still fund the light bill for this place.

Sapphire had a desk in here, a gift from his father and a bed that his mother had bought for him when he slept here.

He placed his backpack on his desk that was covered with paint cans, magazines, miscellaneous paper, and food wrappers.

He walked over to one of his paintings; this one in particular that he looked at was of a woman and a man. The woman had hair like fire and the sun was painted on her forehead. The man had a galaxy and the moon sketched across his chest, his hair short and brown.

He called this painting Fire and Water. It was about two lovers that represented how he viewed love. One over water, the other over fire, both canceling each other out; yet fulfilling each other at the same time.

Thinking of love made him think of Seraphina and thinking of Seraphina made him throw a fireball at the concrete wall.

He screamed as loud as he could and fell to the floor in a very uncomfortable fetal position.

"Why, Seraphina?" he moaned. "Why, Seraphina, why, Seraphina, why? I loved you so much…why?"

As he rested on the concrete floor he looked up at the long light fixtures on the gray ceiling.

He was more furious than he had ever been before. He was about to get his revenge.

5 RAGE

He sat up and stopped crying. His tears didn't mean anything to anyone –not his father, Seraphina or Cerberus. It was no longer time for softness, patience – and love had gone out the window earlier that night.

He rested on his knees as the moonlight peered through the two wide windows at him.

He closed his eyes and whispered, "Grapta Logi Tichos and words appeared all over the walls.

Liar.

Cheater.

Deceiver.

They covered the walls by the hundreds all in black ink. The writings on the wall had become his new wallpaper for his guest that he wanted over.

Now was not the time for being weak, frail or quiet.

Sapphire was angry and when his frustration reached past his breaking point dangerous things would happen. He grabbed his grimoire and found just the spell he was looking for. It was perfect, almost too good to be true.

He read the instructions in his spell book a second time, for assurance. He then took some black chalk that he had on his desk and drew a circle on the ground, big enough for him to sit in. Once finished, he memorized the incantation and sat in the circle (like his grimoire had instructed) and crossed his legs.

He looked straight ahead.

He opened his mouth and said, "Éléso Menos Plisiaka Menos, Éléso Menos Plisiaka Menos," over and over again, and suddenly, the circle of black chalk became a circle of fire, then black smoke, and finally, a ring surrounding him on the ground with glowing Greek letters on its outer rim.

Seraphina and Cerberus were still dancing together at his house party. But as they bounced back and forth, their eyes became still, their bodies stopped moving and they turned their heads towards the front door.

As Sapphire sat, surrounded by the glowing circle, Seraphina and Cerberus began to walk towards the front door. One of Cerberus' friends asked where he was going but he didn't answer as he and Seraphina left his home in synchronized steps, side by side, at the same pace. The two headed for Sapphire and he was waiting for them with devious thoughts flooding his brain.

He had cast a spell to draw them close to him, they couldn't resist.

While the two walked like twin zombies, Sapphire thought of what he was to do with them.

He had plenty of time to decide how he was going to get his revenge.

They didn't know who they had hurt. They didn't know of whom they were dealing with.

He thought on his lover and convinced himself that it was all over. All of the romance. All of the mushy feelings. It was all done.

Sapphire had gotten up, once the circle glowed brighter, an indication that his guests were here. The grimoire mentioned that it would do just that when they were close and he walked out to see them as they continued on towards him.

They didn't speak. Cerberus, with his tall frame, stood by Seraphina and they looked lost, almost dead inside. Where was his cockiness now that he was a human puppet? Sapphire waved his hand at them and their bodies levitated in the air as if an invisible hand held their backs in its palm.

They were in a trance.

They looked pathetic in his sight.

Their bodies followed after him, still hovering in the air as he walked back into the concrete building, the metal door that he had emerged from closing itself.

There were two folding chairs that were on the wall and he made them fly towards the center of the room. Cerberus and Seraphina's bodies slumped into the chairs, their backs touching each other, a rope that was in a barrel wrapped itself around them.

Sapphire took some masking tape that he had on his desk and wrapped it around both their mouths, a smile now forming on his face. He didn't need it because no one would hear them scream where he was, but, he didn't want to hear them speak, he was done with that.

Sapphire put his dreadlocks into a pony tail and picked up a wooden bat that he had on his desk for protection against intruders.

He banged on his cluttered desk five times. Bang, bang, bang, bang, bang. Cerberus and Seraphina blinked their eyes and began to realize just what type of situation they were in. They jumped and shoved but couldn't move. The ropes were tight around their bodies and entangled around their hands. They were tied together, backs facing each other, as close as Sapphire guest that they really wanted to be. If Seraphina wanted to be with him, why would he interfere?

"RISE AND SHINE!" He said as he swung the bat around as if he was practicing for a perfect swing.

Seraphina and Cerberus looked very frightened and that pleased him a great deal. He was in control now.

They were both trying to speak but he couldn't make out a word that they were saying. He couldn't tell who looked more terrified but was just glad that they were.

He put his hand on Seraphina's face, her brown eyes looking up at him sorrowfully.

"Three months," he said as he ran his finger through her hair. "Three whole months it took me to get you that ring that you're wearing. I skipped lunch sometimes. Heck, I even wore the same old MOPPED STAINED shoes until I had gotten it for you. But inside, it really meant nothing to you, huh? You didn't care."

Cerberus was bickering muffled words and Seraphina had tears flowing down her face.

He walked over to a rusted can of paint, "You never cared!" he screamed as he wacked the can off his desk and continued to repeat this behavior while talking. "I had promised to save myself for you, for marriage – I was gonna marry you – and here you are sneaking around with this sorry dog for months. And you couldn't even tell me?" Whack! He smacked his water bottle that he had placed a red rose inside of, "I had to find out from the thug of the month, outside of a trash house party."

Cerberus continued to try and free himself but there was no success. Seraphina wasn't crying silently any more but was now screaming underneath her tight duct tape. Her palms were shaking, her forehead dripping sweat like Cerberus' was.

Seraphina's head bowed as if she had realized how wrong she was for her actions. She looked hurt, guilty, and sorry.

Sapphire sat

"I loved you, girl, do you hear me? I loved you, Seraphina. And you did me dirty?"

There was silence; thickness in the air.

Then, with loud grunting, Sapphire whacked at sculptures, pictures, paintings and bottles of paint that he had all around his desk.

This seemed to make Seraphina cry out in agony, she knew how much he loved his artistic possessions, some of them were gifts from his favorite artists in New York; but at this point, his anger wasn't allowing him to care.

"Cerberus, you had so much in high school," he said as he circled the two, his eyes like a falcon on baby squirrels. "You were the big star, the jock who couldn't miss a shot if he tried. You had girls, money and everyone's attention. Why'd you have to have my girl too? You targeted me for nothing...all I ever wanted to do was enjoy the high school experience – make friends, learn things. They said it would be fun, but they never said you'd be there. You tortured me for four years and then after we graduated you had to have my girl too?"

Sapphire looked Cerberus deep in his eyes; he didn't fear him, even if he wasn't in ropes. He raised his hand and Seraphina and Cerberus rose in their seats, still tied together. He made them go round and round in a circle as he cackled.

"I was broken; something inside of me was crippled when you began your reign of punishment on me! I thought I wasn't good enough, you see, that's what bullying does to a person; it makes them feel less of a HUMAN BEING. I had to take medication to keep me from severing you in half with my magic, I had to miss so many days of school to keep myself from destroying you."

He lowered his hand and the two hit the floor with a loud bang as they both were crying. Seraphina was terrified of what he would do and Cerberus was terrified because of what he could do.

"Since you and Seraphina are so close I'm sure she told you of my powers?" Cerberus looked confused as tears ran down his cheeks. "Oh, well I guess not. I'm a warlock, baby boy. I'VE GOT MAGIC IN MY VEINS!"

Sapphire stood in between Cerberus and Seraphina, his head in the middle as he looked ready to swing at any minute. "I'm angry, Cerberus if you can't tell by now. I'm fed up and I need to take my aggression out on someone." He took his bat and slowly shoved it in Cerberus' face. "Do you know what I'm gonna do to you two, huh? I'm gonna beat the brains out of you, well, maybe just Seraphina, since you have none, Cerberus. Or, maybe I'll start with your jaw, yeah I'll bust your mouth up real good since you've got so much of it. HUH!?"

Seraphina muffled a slight "please," as Sapphire swung his bat around.

Cerberus was balling like a child as he realized just

41

how powerless he was in this situation.

"Look around, Seraphina," Sapphire barked as he looked at the writings on the walls. "Liar, cheater, deceiver, these are all the things that you are to me now. You don't deserve my mercy. You know how hateful, how cruel he was to me? Out of everyone in the world you had to cheat on me with him. And I came to you for shelter after my own father had been blasted out for his cheatin', and you still didn't feel the need to confess to me. You do not love me, Seraphina, and I'm done with you."

Sapphire raised his bat at the two but before he could take a swing, he stopped. Flashes of advice, warnings, teachings, and lessons from his family flooded his thoughts. His mother would never approve of what he was doing; he wasn't brought up to be like this. He imagined what his grandparents would say to him if they knew of his doings. He wasn't a kidnapper, he wasn't a murderer, and he wasn't crazy.

He remembered the way his mother and father looked at him as he stood on top of the car he had busted up. They looked at him like he was a monster that needed to be in a cage. He wasn't crazy. He didn't even want to do this, any of this, they made him do it. This wasn't him

The bat hit the concrete.

Sapphire stood still, facing them.

He just looked at the both of them as they didn't know whether to keep begging for mercy or scream.

"I...I'm not...like this...this isn't me. What am I doing? Seraphina, look at me!" Sapphire rushed to Seraphina and bended his knees down to look at her. "You know I'm not like this. I'm not crazy. I just...

I'm just hurting inside... I...just...."

He backed away from them both and looked around at his disaster that he had created with his bat. His art was destroyed. The only thing that was standing was his painting of the two lovers.

He turned back to face Cerberus and Seraphina.

"I'm...I'm gonna let you two go. I'm gonna do it."

He was fighting so many decisions right now. He was scared to let them free but he was scared to keep them here. He wasn't supposed to be the one in fear.

"I'm gonna let you two go before I really HURT you, because believe me I do wanna hurt you two so much. But I want you out of my sight. Seraphina don't call, page or ever come see me. We're over. And if you two as so much whisper a word of our little encounter I will find out and torture the living souls out of you, I swear it! Do you understand me?"

The two shook their heads like wimpy children and suddenly the ropes released them. They ripped off their tape and breathed out of their mouths for the first time in half an hour. Cerberus, without saying anything, ran away as if Sapphire was his worst nightmare. But Seraphina didn't go anywhere.

She just looked at him. More tears. More whimpering.

"GOOOOOO!" Sapphire hollered, his voice making her jump.

It was truly over. Everything they had built together in their relationship was gone. Sapphire's heart ached so badly. His spirit was crushed. This was how he said his good bye.

Seraphina ran off, her long hair flapping at her back.

An hour had passed and Sapphire sat on the

concrete with just his black boxers on. He was making himself a potion as he thought on all the things that had just happened.

He had taken two people under his control without their knowledge, threatened to harm them and then set them free.

6 ARSON

He was furious that he had let them leave without a scratch, but wasn't going to do another spell to bring them back.

Now, he had an even more maleficent plan. He was making a potion that was listed as an anti-flame concoction. He hadn't been a master at potions but had been experimenting in his room on a few. He had all the ingredients that he needed already around; this potion didn't require a lot.

He didn't have a cauldron around so he took an empty paint can and set it down on the floor.

With the help of his grimoire's instructions, he poured a bottle of water that he had into the paint can. He then took some dirt and sprinkled it into the can. Next, the potion required three drops of tears, and while he bent over to look at the water, they were already dripping down his face and into the can, causing the potion to bubble. He needed to stir for thirty seconds and add the final ingredient which was a strand of hair and he easily plucked one from his dreadlocks and placed it into the water that had now become the color of cream soda.

His strand of hair dissolved into the potion and after Sapphire had stirred it for thirty more seconds it was ready for him to apply to his body.

The potion had the texture of baby oil. Sapphire rubbed it in, spreading it all around his chest, torso, arms and down to his legs. He was ready After smearing the rest of it on his face.

Sapphire was going to teleport. He had been practicing on it, but didn't like when he regurgitated after, so he barely worked on the craft. Despite his doubts of being successful without emptying out his insides, he still had to carry out his mission, so he closed his eyes and focused on the location that he wanted to be in.

After five seconds of deep concentration, he had vanished into a puff of black smoke.

He hated teleportation as much as he hated rollercoasters and didn't know which one felt worse. He couldn't see anything but could hear a ringing in his ears – and nothing was under his feet. This was a terrible experience. He was moving very fast and tried hard to concentrate, but that was becoming more and more difficult. Teleporting across the room was a breeze, like blinking his eyes, but ripping through time and space to get to a distant location made him feel as if he was in a whirlwind.

Finally, he could see again.

Sapphire was now in his old high school, Ravin High. He knew that no one would be here at 2:00.am so he wasn't worried about being in just his boxers.

He hadn't been here since graduation and never wanted to come back. He was happy to do creative writing and acting here but each hall way reminded him of how hard it was to have a peaceful day when Cerberus stomped through them.

He walked down the hall of lockers that he was tortured in and continued down to a round room that had trophies stacked high in a glass case. Around the walls were young men that had been very successful in their years, but every trophy in the case belonged to Cerberus. He was the schools most accomplished athlete.

Even after two years, the school basketball team had not won any major games, according to Seraphina who still continued to come visit her fellow lower-classmen. Cerberus was their only hope for wins.

He had lost his most prized possessions to him so it was time that the tables were flipped. Cerberus would brag about these trophies to everyone almost every day in school.

He destroyed Sapphire's hope so he was going to destroy his shrine. He was going to burn it all.

With his hands raised above his head, Sapphire whispered, "Enkarmos," and the trophy cabinet became engulfed with bright, crackling fire. Its contents burned inside as he stood, motionless, just looking down.

He had completed half of his mission but there was still more to do.

As he inhaled the satisfying smell of the burning trophies, Sapphire pointed his hand at the flaming, glass cabinet and said, "Anaxinxo." The fire began to grow, almost touching the ceiling. Sapphire put his hands back up in the air and yelled, "Anaxinxo!"

Suddenly, the flames grew and surrounded the entire trophy room. Sapphire couldn't feel the heat but could see its damage on the pictures on the walls, each of them melting. He heard the fire alarms but that didn't stop him from continuing on. He was angry and if he couldn't physically harm anyone he was going to at least take his frustration out on material things.

He walked out of the burning trophy room and looked to his left and then his right. He remembered one day that he was walking on the west wing of the hall and had been shoved into a locker by Cerberus for doing absolutely nothing. He looked to the east wing on his right and saw a trash can that he swore he was thrown in; it was still here to remind him of his despair.

Sapphire thought about all the nights he would cry because he couldn't stomach the idea of going to school another day just to be hurt. Seeing this school as he passed by sometimes would make his heart ache. He hated to look upon it. But now he was here and he was going to put an end to it, all the memories even the ones with Seraphina, he was going to burn.

He made the flames spread out from the trophy room, and as they licked the floor they reflecting brightly against his oily body. He looked to his left and shot the fire down the hall way and it licked everything in its path, while he did the same to the right side of the school. The sprinklers had started to burst out but they were no match for the fire that he had continued to grow.

He had one more hallway that wasn't burning up and that was the one directly in front of him. He closed his eyes for a second and convinced himself that finishing this would give him closure. He forced the fire to fly after him as he ran through the hall. He felt free. He felt accomplished. This was a spiritual thing for him, this was a healing situation.

He was releasing. All the frustration, all the hurt, all the anxiety. He was setting it free. The boy who had once been the slave to adolescent abuse was now a new creature; a free creature.

As he ran through the hallway he looked alive. The fire followed after him, very swiftly, as he spread his arms wide, looking as if he was a majestic eagle. He turned a corner and the roaring flames followed.

The hallway was completely set ablaze. He stood in the center as red and yellow flashes adorned his face. He wasn't scared to be surrounded by this fire, it didn't hurt him, it wanted to obey him, he could feel it.

"Weeeeeooooooooweeeeeeooo."

That seemed to snap Sapphire out of his mood. He turned to his left, hearing what sounded like two fire trucks heading his way. He had to leave.

He couldn't be seen here. He was the only one in the school, surrounded by all of this blazing fire. He could go to jail if caught here.

He became very frightened, breathing hard. It was time to leave but he felt so weak inside as he tried to calm his heart rate. Teleporting took lots of strength and his magic had been used on incinerating his high school.

Still, he had to try. He had to go. There were no cameras in Ravin High, because there was not enough drama that required them. Sapphire wasn't afraid of being on camera but couldn't be bothered by a fire fighter.

He closed his eyes and thought of his painting room. As he heard the fire trucks get closer he vanished into a puff of black smoke but had instantly lost focus as the fear of his consequences rushed through him. What had he done? A whole school was set ablaze because of him. Many wouldn't have a place to learn, a free lunch or a warm class room to be educated in. And he had practically kidnapped before that.

And his father's car was damaged at the hands of him. He wasn't like this, he wasn't a cruel person.

Sapphire opened his eyes but was not inside of his painting room any more. Now he was in a large parking garage.

He was scared. Failing at teleportation could be very severe. His mother had warned him that some magicians had ended up on islands, in the ocean or even a volcano, in the past.

There were only a few cars in the spacious garage and he wondered if anyone was going to see him so oily, in nothing but his boxers.

He was so exhausted that he sat against the back of a golden van, leaning his head on its glass. In tears, he slid down and put his face in his hands.

He was in so much trouble. More trouble than he had been in before he had left his father's home. What was wrong with his life?

"What am I gonna do?" He whispered.

"You can take my hand," said a gentle voice.

7 HOPE

Sapphire looked up to see a man with light skin and a thick, curly afro standing in front of him. He had on a brown, fur coat and tight, burgundy slacks. Leopard print shoes were on his feet and he had on a beaded necklace with alligator teeth in it.

"I didn't think you'd be half naked?" The man said, his hand stretching out to Sapphire. "Calypso should have drawn the whole scene instead of just from the neck up."

"I'm sorry, I don't know what you're talking about," Sapphire said as he felt weird about being in front of another man with just his boxers on.

"Oh, excuse me, I'm so rude," the man said with a shy smile. "My name's Leonidas."

"What can I help you with?"

Did he want money?

"No, I'm here to help you, Sapphire."

"What? How do you know my name?" Sapphire squinted his eyes. "What do you want?"

"Look, you've had a long night, I know, I can understand why you're a little frantic but if you'd just let me have a moment of your time I'm sure I'd be able to help you."

Leonidas took off his fur coat, knelt down to Sapphire and wrapped it around his chilled body, "I know you're cold. I've got a warm room waiting on you. And if you haven't eaten I've got two refrigerators full of food."

Sapphire felt the warmth that the fur coat had given him. He stood up as Leonidas lifted him to his feet. He seemed nice, but he wasn't sure of what his intentions were with him.

As Leonidas stood in just a tank top he placed his left hand over Sapphire's shoulder and said, "I'm just like you, a magician. You have nothing to be worried about. I mean absolutely no harm. Just trust me; I know I'm a stranger, but if you'd just walk and talk with me for a moment, I promise that it will do you some good."

"You ain't no creep, are you?" Sapphire asked.

"I'm a fellow magician who wants to help."

"How do you know my name?"

"My friend, Calypso, is psychic. She has visions about stuff. She saw that you'd be here...before you were here. She helps me find all of the magicians that are in need."

"Okay...and you...and her live together?"

"Me and all of the other magicians that we help."

Leonidas smiled but Sapphire kept his still expression as he gripped his fur coat.

"Come on, walk with me, talk with me, I'd let you ride in my car but it's in the shop until next week. If you think I'm a creep would a creep do this?" Leonidas kicked off his leopard print shoes and gestured for Sapphire to put them on.

"I'm not gonna take your shoes," Sapphire said.

"You can give em back once we get to Boon Hood," Leonidas said. "And I'm gonna need that fur coat back too, man. That was my mother's."

Sapphire felt the cold concrete floor that was under his feet. It wasn't freezing out but November's weather gave off a chill that made the ground very unpleasant.

"I'll look so silly walking in just leopard shoes and a fur coat," Sapphire said.

"What, you want my pants too?" Leonidas asked.

"No...no, I'm fine. I'll put them on."

"We can take a short cut through an alley way so cars won't see you. But once we get to Boon Hood the other's outside their apartments might see you."

"What's Boon Hood?"

"I'll tell you if you just come on with me. You're in despair and you need a home, and...hope. Calypso could see all of that in her crystal ball."

"Okay, I'll come with you. But I can throw fire balls really fast. If you try anything stupid you might regret it." Sapphire looked at Leonidas very seriously as the wind blew through his dreadlocks.

He really wanted to be inside four falls. It seemed to be getting colder the longer they stood in the parking garage.

"Okay, you have my word that I won't harm you," Leonidas said. "Now come on."

"Prove to me that you're a magician."

Leonidas grinned as he looked at Sapphire's untrusting eyes. He lifted his hands as if he was holding an invisible globe and said, "Imagingo Akananana."

A figure of a panda eating bamboo appeared; looking as if it were made up of stars or maybe even tiny pixels. Was it a hologram, Sapphire wondered, or was Leonidas really a magician like he said that he was?

"Okay, that's cool," said Sapphire as Leonidas made the panda do a summersault in his palm.

Sapphire slowly followed Leonidas as he walked out of the parking garage and into the night.

"Am I still in Harlem?" he asked.

"Of course," said Leonidas, "we're just about to go to a little neighborhood that I live in called Boon Hood. You can tell me all about your story on the way. It's not far but it is a walk."

"Okay," Sapphire said as he continued to walk with Leonidas. "Well, I...I've been through a rough night."

"How rough?" asked Leonidas.

"Very rough. I burned – I mean, never mind."

"What?"

"Nothing."

"You can tell me your story, Sapphire," Leonidas said as he turned a corner and walked through an abandoned park. "You can trust me, my dude."

"I just did some bad stuff," said Sapphire. "I was hurt really badly by my girl, Seraphina."

"Mmmm, Seraphina, she sounds hot."

"She cheated on me."

"Oh," said Leonidas, scrunching up his face.

"Yeah, Prince was right; the beautiful ones hurt you every time. And before I found that out, my parents had got into a bad fight because my dad was cheating, too."

"Das crazy," Leonidas whispered.

"Yup."

"So, you've got a lot on your heart right now, huh?"

"Yeah, and after I beat the snot out of my dad's car I moved out. I couldn't stay under his roof any more, or my girls. Then, I got into some mess and tried to teleport out of it and ended up –"

"You can teleport?" asked Leonidas.

"Sure," said Sapphire. "But I hate doing it. I feel so nauseous afterwards."

"Man...I can't teleport at all. No one ever showed me. And no one at the apartment can. The magic I learned is all from scraps of pages that my Papa left behind from his grimoire."

"Hey, I have a grimoire."

"You do!?" Leonidas asked, his face full of excitement.

"Yeah, but it's back at this place...where I paint. A lot of my stuff is."

"Wow...do you know how rare it is to come across a grimoire?" Leonidas asked. "That's probably why you're so good at teleportation, you've got a whole manual on that kind of stuff."

"Yeah, I've learned a lot of spells from it. It's my baby."

Leonidas turned another corner as Sapphire followed behind. They were on a dim street, passing by a gas station that was full of hooded men and women that passed cigarettes and insults at one another.

"Do you think you can let us see it...maybe tomorrow when you've gotten your strength back...you could get it for us?" Leonidas asked.

"Sure." Sapphire said.

"Everybody back at the apartment will be so happy when they get to learn new spells. I've been tryna' get them to learn my voodoo magic but they can't really get a grip on it. It's really powerful stuff."

"Voodoo?" Sapphire said.

"Yup, I am a voodoo magician. I use the power of my ancestors to cast my spells. It makes em way stronger and keeps me from losing my energy."

"Oh I just hate that. When you cast a few spells and feel like you need to rest for two days straight."

"Ha! Man, but you've probably got all kinds of spells, Sapphire. Spells I've probably never even heard of. Maybe you can teach us...it's about time we all learn new magic. You see, Sapphire, I own an apartment and five other magicians live their too. I use my apartment as a shelter for magical folk that need a family...a place to rest their heads and three meals a day."

"That's really cool...that you do that," Sapphire said as he noticed Leonidas was leading him on a street where many people were crowded around cars and motorcycles.

"And you can stay as long as you'd like." Leonidas announced. "No charge for magicians...my mother would turn over in her grave if she ever knew that I was charging magicians to live with me. She started the whole shelter in our apartment, back in 1969."

Sapphire was listening to Leonidas but his attention was focusing more on two women who were leaning against a brown town car. They winked at him, both of them wearing blond wigs, colored leotards and cheetah print coats. It was dark out but the bright street lights were revealing a neighborhood, where what appeared to be prostitutes, hung out

"Hey, King Leonidas," said one of the women in a blond wig.

"Hey, Andromeda," said Leonidas as Sapphire looked around and observed his surroundings. He wondered where Leonidas was leading him. And why did that woman call him a king? Who was he?

A raggedy, old man with gray bristles on his head

and a long trench coat bowed to his knee when Sapphire and Leonidas walked past him.

"Hey, Nicoleto, how many times do I have to tell you to stop bowing to me?" Leonidas asked with a grin.

"I'll always give honor to whom honor is due, King Leonidas," said the old man, with a faint grin.

"He does that every time he sees me," Leonidas said.

"You're a king?" Sapphire asked as he looked at Leonidas.

"Yeah, my dad is the son of a Nigerian king...and after he died he became king and then when he died I was his only son to take his throne."

In a neighborhood where gangs and prostitutes seemed to populate the area, Sapphire didn't think he'd be walking around with a king. Leonidas walked further in the middle of the street and stopped. "Mr. Sapphire, sir," Leonidas said with his hands raised, "welcome to Boon Hood."

Sapphire and Leonidas stood in the middle of the street and on both sides were two three story apartments that all faced each other. Groups of people were in the middle of the street drinking, laughing, smoking and playing loud music out of their cars.

Leonidas led Sapphire to an older man with chubby cheeks and a black over coat on to match his flat cap. He sat at a table with hats of all sorts. On a rack by him were coats of many different lengths and on his left was a burgundy van with many warm clothing items on display in the back.

"Hey, Donatello," Leonidas said as he walked up to the man. "You out here this late? Still on the grind, huh?"

"Sho' nuff," said Donatello, his pop eyes looking at Sapphire's attire.

"This is Sapphire," Leonidas said, pointing his thumb, "he's my main man, can you get 'em some gear?"

"Anything for the kings men. Free of charge as always, I'm not taking your money, Leonidas. What you got in mind?"

Leonidas looked over all of Donatello's goods and then back over at Sapphire. "I like this black fedora hat, it'll look good on you, Sapphire. Oh, and these black slacks."

Leonidas took some black slacks from the table and handed them to Sapphire who was glad to cover his legs with them. He then took a black, wide brimmed hat and placed it over his dreadlocks that were still in a ponytail. Next, Leonidas handed him a blue sweater to cover his back.

"It's complete. Perfect!" Leonidas said as he tilted Sapphire's black hat just a smidge for style.

The two headed towards the apartment on the left side.

"This apartment is named after my father, Osiris. And the three others are named after his three friends. Sapphire looked at the apartment that Leonidas was leading him to and then at the one across from it. Two more identical apartments were across the street facing them. Three men that wore wheat colored coats all waved at Leonidas who returned their greeting with a piece sign.

"Who's that with you, Leonidas?" One of them asked.

"His name's Sapphire," said Leonidas, "he's gonna

be staying with us for a while."

Leonidas walked to the bright red door of the apartment and it opened by itself, revealing the first floor hall with a long, wooden table in it, eight wooden chairs on both sides of it and a higher, oak chair at the head if it. On both sides of the hall were four doors.

"This is the dining hall; we have three meals a day here. In the morning everybody comes down for breakfast and we share anything we want to release off our chest. Then, everybody just does whatever they want after that – oh, but tomorrow we're doing talent night in my room, upstairs. It's just a time for us to express our art and kick it, it helps us get all the frustration out of our minds."

Leonidas took off his fur coat from Sapphire and gestured for him to walk up the steps that led to the second floor.

"My mom enchanted that door downstairs to open every time a magician comes near," said Leonidas. "She wanted all magical folk to feel welcomed. This was all her idea, like I said, to open our apartment building for homeless magicians. Now, I want you to meet every one, they should still be up."

Sapphire walked down the hall and followed after Leonidas who walked towards the first door. He knocked and it opened itself.

A black woman with long ankle length braids was meditating in her room that had pink walls and mask hung up on them. She was hovering two feet off the floor with her eyes closed. In her apartment room were many candles that floated behind.

She opened one eye to look at Sapphire and Leonidas, "hey, babe," she said as she winked at

Sapphire. "We all made pizza's and there's still a lot of it left down stairs, if he's hungry, Leonidas."

"Okay," said Leonidas, his hands on Sapphire's shoulders. "This is my best friend, Calypso. She's the one who knew you were in trouble."

"Cool," said Sapphire. "I've never met a psychic."

"Yeah, it's a blessing and a curse," Calypso said as she now hovered upside down like a bat, her meditation position still held.

"Now I've got to get back to my meditating...I'll chit chat with you two hunks in the morning. I'm making French toast and eggs."

"My favorite," Sapphire said.

"I know," Calypso whispered as her door closed itself.

Next Leonidas went to the adjacent door and knocked. Suddenly, it flung open and a light skinned, young man with ear length dreadlocks was blasting 2pac Shakur on his stereo. He was dancing to it but not on the floor, instead, he was breakdancing on his wall.

"Whoa," said Sapphire as the young man jumped off the wall and walked over to them. He had on a leather jacket with black leather slacks and a tattoo on his neck that said Southside.

That must've hurt, Sapphire thought as he stretched out his hand to shake his. Leonidas introduced him as Cirrus.

"What's good, bruv?" Cirrus said as he plucked his finger at the top of Sapphire's black hat. "You lookin' mad fresh."

"Thank you," Sapphire said.

"You're looking at one of the greatest rappers around," said Leonidas as he pointed at Cirrus.

"Nah, nobody will ever be greater than the almighty Pac," said Cirrus as Sapphire looked in his room at all of the 2Pac posters that were plastered on his wall.

These apartments were small. He guessed that they were all studio apartments.

"We gone let you get back to dancing, bro bro," said Leonidas. "I'm gone try to introduce Sapphire to everyone and then we're gonna go check out the pizza's y'all made."

"Yeah, we made PEPPERONI, all of them, extra pepperoni. Calypso said it was his favorite so we made like eight of 'em. There's so much of it left."

"That's my girl. Always being so welcoming," Leonidas said as Cirrus closed his door.

Next, Leonidas introduced Sapphire to a Caucasian girl with a blond bob. He said her name was Neptune and she waved at Sapphire as she watched Television. Her room was covered in neon blue Christmas lights that adorned her walls and windows. She was lounging on a her bed with a bag of potato chips in her hand. She wore a white halter top and black leather pants.

"He's cute," said Neptune as she nonchalantly waved her hand and her door closed itself. She wasn't very welcoming but Sapphire didn't care, he was so excited to be around other magicians that seemed to be just as creative as he was. Leonidas knocked on a door across the hall to Neptune's but no one answered. After knocking three times, Leonidas waved his hand and the door opened itself.

"He stays sleep," said Leonidas as Sapphire could see an arm hanging from underneath a blanket that was covering a face.

"That's my little homie, Othello," said Leonidas. "He's an excellent hip hop dancer. He's the youngest out of all of us. He's nineteen, but I found him when he was sixteen. Every one's been here for about three years."

"How old are you?" Sapphire asked as Leonidas closed Othello's door.

"I'm twenty eight and, Calypso's thirty. Cirrus is twenty five and Neptune and Napoleon are twenty four – oh you've got to meet Napoleon."

Leonidas walked over to the last door and pointed at it. As the door opened, a Caucasian man was resting on his knees as a guitar in front of him was on fire. He was growing the fire with his fingers and behind him was loud heavy metal music that was playing ferociously.

Sapphire wondered why he was doing this. Was he on drugs?

"Hey, Napoleon," Leonidas said as the Caucasian man ran his hand over his long blond hair, moving it so he could see Sapphire better.

"This is Sapphire, he's gonna be staying with us."

"Alright!" said Napoleon as he jumped over his flaming guitar and shook Sapphire's hand. "Your name rocks!"

"Thank you," said Sapphire. "What are you doing to your guitar?"

"I burn it…every now and then. You know."

"Oh," Sapphire said in a whisper.

He thought this was a very vague explanation.

Everyone seemed so extraordinary to him, so different. In school, he had always been made fun of for being different from others but now everyone in the apartment seemed to be oozing with individual uniqueness. He thought of living here, life wouldn't be so bad with these magicians. He liked all of them, even the boy under the blanket sounded easy to get along with.

"I wanna take you up stairs to the throne room," said Leonidas. As he walked up the steps, Sapphire following behind. "I give everyone that moves in a little history of what we do, who I am, and how this all happened."

Leonidas led Sapphire up to the third and final floor. At the top was a long hall with the same amount of doors as the other but at the end was a high, wooden throne with all sorts of odd items around it.

"This is my throne room. My rooms to the right." Leonidas looked up at pictures that were on the wall. The large one that he was glaring at was of a black man with corn rows and the same exact necklace that Leonidas was wearing. He looked dignified, maybe even haughty. "King Osiris, I'm not half the man my pops was…but I try."

Leonidas turned to Sapphire as he asked, "so, you and your father come from royalty?"

"Yes," said Leonidas, as he walked up three wooden steps that were before his throne. He sat on it and rested his arms.

On the steps of Leonidas's throne were odd figures that made Sapphire perplexed. There was a donkey tail, rabbit's foot, horse shoe, acorns and a golden figurine of a small lion all on the thrones steps. There was also candles, of all colors, on the steps as well.

"We come from royal, magical stock," said Leonidas. "In Nigeria, in 1948, my great grandparents were King and Queen of a rich land, powerful magicians they were. They ruled for many years until the day that my great grandfather had gotten into a fight with his younger brother, Ojijio. He wanted the kingdom and thought my grandfather was too weak to rule. He ambushed his kingdom, Ojijio did, after being exiled from the kingdom for his disrespect."

Sapphire listened very carefully as Leonidas spoke. He was getting history on African culture, something he treasured deeply.

"Ojijio murdered my great grandfather and his son and his son's wife," said Leonidas, "with his army that he had formed from his own comrades. They overcame his men and him as well. My great grandmother, Chimamonda, escaped with her grandson, Osiris, and her maid, and fled to America as a refugee. They were able to come to New York, and they searched around for a home to raise Osiris in."

"And Osiris is your father?" asked Sapphire.

"Right," said Leonidas. "Chimamonda and her maid came across an apartment in Harlem. She saw families out on the apartment steps playing and enjoying each other's company. She thought within herself that this had to be the best place to raise my father. She needed a home and he needed a family. Her maid interpreted for her and asked the five families that stayed in the apartment building if they could provide a home for them with the promise that Chimamonda would use her magic to heal any of their children's illnesses, keeping them all in good health."

Sapphire's eyes lit up as Leonidas spoke. This was like an epic poem; the way he spoke was even in a poetic rhythm. "So they let her stay with them?" he asked.

"Yup," said Leonidas. "The Sphinx's, a lovely family in an upper room let them stay with them. Chimamonda's maid told them all that she was not only a queen but that her magic was real – and she proved it to them by healing their children of any ailments that they had. She was a skilled voodoo magician but her strengths were only in healing."

Like my mom, thought Sapphire.

"Because of Chimamonda's power and love, the tenants in the apartment would all bring her food, portions of money – they loved her and called her Queen Chimamonda! She raised her grandson, Osiris, around the four families own son's: Aristotle, Pierre, River and Saturn. They all grew up together and everyone called him King Osiris. He had grown up to be a powerful young man, a superior spell caster at just the age of eighteen – Isn't that magnificent?"

"What's a superior spell caster?" Sapphire asked.

"A magician with very strong powers – able to do great things! Osiris was the leader of the other boys, always getting them out of dangerous situations with his magic. The sons of the tenants had all started to drift off into hustling and the pigs were riding their backs hard."

"Hustling?"

"Yeah, they sold drugs. But they had no choice. The factory that their fathers had worked at had closed down, and whites in the 50's and 60's weren't passing out much work to dark skinned people. They used the money they had to support their families but the youngest boy of the group never really wanted part in it; but he tagged along with them anyway.

Things were fine, money was flowing, but one day, in 1968, the pigs got in the way."

"The cops?" Said Sapphire, in a whisper.

"Yes the cops...." said Leonidas. "Racist and foul white devil's that roamed the streets looking for a young black man to bring to his knees." Leonidas slapped his hand on his right throne arm. "They harassed my father and his boys, and kidnapped Saturn when he was walking by himself one night…and hung him. Just…just because they could. When King Osiris found out he was furious – he took care of them both, getting revenge for Saturn ."

"Whoa," whispered Sapphire, his hands gripping on to each other.

"My father searched all through Harlem until he could find a place to relocate his three remaining friends and their families, and came across these four apartment buildings. He compelled the three to go over their money's and each of them were asked to purchase one of these apartments. Osiris bought this one but was so sad that his grandmother couldn't come, she was already in a nursing home – too old to move around – and her maid had died years before.

Osiris declared, on the day that he and his friends had purchased these four apartments, that they could sell and trade without the pigs stopping their hustle. He offered them protection and they each gave him a portion of their earnings, satisfied that they had a leader – a king – who could keep them safe from the Man."

"Amazing," said Sapphire as he looked back over at the picture of Osiris. He could see why he looked so dignified.

"On December the 13th," said Leonidas, "the day

that they had all moved into the four apartments, King Osiris had a feast here. He said that on the 13th of December, every year, the four leaders of the families would host a special feast and celebrate at one of their apartment buildings.

"He called this feast the Brethren Gathering. I was just a baby then, he had met my mother, Jasperella, a year before – a sweet Latino girl from New Jersey. He named this neighborhood Boon Hood because it was a very beneficial place for us all."

"That's incredible," said Sapphire. "He created all of this on his own."

"Yup, the whole system was his idea, but, the shelter was my mother's."

"Sapphire looked at a picture of a Latino girl with a young infant in her hands, he guessed that she had to be Leonidas's mother; he had her eyes.

"The other three apartments were full of their families but ours just had us," said Leonidas. "My mother begged my father to open our home up for a shelter for homeless magicians – and he did – but they could only find three in need."

Leonidas pointed over to a picture of three young girls posing with his mother who looked very pleased to be in the company of other magical women like herself.

"So, you kept her tradition of the shelter for magicians?" asked Sapphire. "That's great. But where are your parents now?"

"My mother lost her battle to heart failure because my father couldn't find an internal healing potion for her. Then, when I was twenty he died of cancer. I guess...smoking cancer sticks helped him cope with my mother's death, but couldn't help keep him healthy. On his last day as king, while on his death bed, he told me that I would have to take over the throne. That's why all these charms are here."

Sapphire looked at all of the diverse items around Leonidas's throne.

"What do they do?"

"The donkey tail, rabbits foot, and candles bring good luck," said Leonidas. "The horseshoe, acorns and that gold lion ward off bad luck – and the spirits of diabetes, cancer and heart disease are afraid of Jack-o-lanterns. These were all Calypso's idea."

"You're trying to escape death?"

"I'm trying to avoid death," said Leonidas, "as long as I can. I've been keeping up the traditions of my family for a long time and I can't do it with bad health. The other leaders of the three apartments passed their business down to their children as well, to birth a new generation. Alexandrite owns the one across from us, and over across the street, Crystal and Machiavelli take charge in their apartments."

"It's like a whole underground government!" said Sapphire. "This is brilliant."

"Yup," Leonidas said as he hopped off his throne.

"You said that Calypso helps you find magicians, right?" asked Sapphire as Leonidas nodded. "Did you help her too?"

"Her mother, Cleopatra, was one of the magicians here. She left her here when she was just two...to go back to her life as a...prostitute. Me and her grew up together and she not only uses her psychic abilities to find the magicians I need, but cooks and cleans around here. She's so sweet."

Leonidas pointed his hand towards the left side of the wall and Sapphire beheld five paintings that moved him in a way he couldn't describe.

The paintings were of the five magicians that Leonidas had opened his home to and the one that really caught Sapphire's attention was the one of his oily face in the parking garage. He was looking up to a hand, Leonidas's hand.

"Calypso can paint very well," said Leonidas. "We both enjoy the arts. She searches her crystal ball almost every morning for the homeless. When she finds one, she paints them, just like she saw them in the vision and tells me exactly where they'll be when I come for them...to comfort them and give them hope."

"I love paintings so much," said Sapphire. "My favorite painter is Basquiat. I try to be as good and as free as he is with his work, but I don't think I'll ever line up to him, Leonidas."

"I've heard of him," said Leonidas. "He's the guy with the weird hair.... He passed away, didn't he?"

"Yeah, drug addiction" said Sapphire. "But...his art lives on....Forever."

Besides the picture of Sapphire, the other paintings were just as brilliant. There was one of a black boy with corn rows and he was sprawled out on a bus seat with bruises on his body.

"I found Othello after his mother kicked him out...because he didn't like her abusive boyfriend."

"People are so cruel," said Sapphire.

"Cirrus was about to be shot by his older brother before I intercepted, Neptune was about to be taken advantage of by two guys after walking to a women's shelter she stayed in, and Napoleon – well, he was about to finish himself off before I came through."

"Finish himself off?" said Sapphire.

"Yeah he was going to shoot himself cause his home had just went into foreclosure," said Leonidas. "He thought I was an angel when I broke down his door. But I'm no angel."

"Are you gonna pass this down to your kids one day?"

"I don't know if I want kids. Besides, I already have my baby."

Leonidas walked over to a glass cage that was in the middle of the hall way. He pulled out a dark green, black spotted boa constrictor and hung it over his neck.

"This is my baby right here; she's quiet and doesn't ask too many annoying questions like children do."

"She's pretty," said Sapphire as he reached out a hand to feel the skin of the reptile. Half of him wanted to hold it and the other half didn't fight the idea. "What's her name?"

"Nekita," said Leonidas as he lifted his snake. "Here," he said as he lowered Nekita over Sapphire's neck. "It was a gift for my birthday...I got her two years ago from my best friend, Machiavelli."

"Whoa, whoa," Sapphire said as he felt how heavy the constrictor was on his shoulders.

"She's a sweetheart, she won't bite you. Trust me."

After a few more minutes of talking with Leonidas, Sapphire ate pizza with him and he elaborated more on his dramatic story of being betrayed. Leonidas listened, and that's exactly what he needed that night.

After receiving his room key from Leonidas, Sapphire told him that he would be glad to stay until he could get back on his feet. He was no longer returning to his job, in the hopes of finding something better any way.

But until then, this new place would be his. Boon Hood was his new home. Boon Hood was his new hope.

8 BROTHERHOOD

The apartment that he was given was room 207, at the end of the hall, across from Napoleon. Sapphire slept on a lumpy bed and wrote poetry on paper that Leonidas had left him with.

There was nothing inside his apartment room but a bed and a desk with a lamp on it. There was a kitchen right next to the bathroom and he thought they were both well styled. He liked architecture.

He would often tell people that his favorite part of being a New Yorker was getting to see the massive buildings that sprung from the ground like concrete trees. To him they represented power.

He awoke with the smell of his favorite breakfast, French toast, and eggs, flowing throughout the three halls of Osiris. After showering, he heard a knock on his door. He slipped into his pants that Leonidas had given him and opened his door with a slight crack.

It was Calypso, in a red sweater and a beaded band around her long braids.

Here you go, honey," she said as she handed Sapphire three shopping bags of socks, shoes, boxers, miscellaneous toiletries, a few sweaters and two pairs of jeans.

"Thank you," Sapphire said.

"No problem...just a lil something to welcome you to the apartment," said Calypso. "Come downstairs when you're ready to eat. I've made a big breakfast."

"Sure, thank you so much, Calypso."

And after that, Sapphire closed his door and looked through his items. He dressed quickly, not wanting his food to be cold.

He walked out of his apartment and headed to the first floor to see everyone eating at the dining table. He noticed that Leonidas was sitting at the head of the table and he smiled as he saw Sapphire come down.

"Good morning," said Leonidas.

"Mornin'," Sapphire said. Everyone was sitting, speaking through chomps of French toast that was covering an entire plate in the center of the table. Calypso came from the apartment kitchen with two pitchers of juice, one orange the other lemonade.

"We've got a seat for you right by Othello," said Leonidas as he stretched his hand out towards a caramel skinned boy with straight back braids. He had on a white T and blue jeans.

"This is who was knocked out last night," Leonidas said as Sapphire sat next to Othello who dapped hands with him.

On Leonidas's left side of the table was Cirrus (in a black patent leather jacket) Othello and Sapphire; and on the right was Napoleon, Neptune, and Calypso who had just walked over to place a glass cup in front of Sapphire.

"Lemonade or orange juice?" she asked.

"Um, Lemonade, please," said Sapphire, with a

smile, as Calypso poured his beverage.

"She's like everyone's Mama here," Othello said as he nudged Sapphire's elbow. "And she's just as bossy as one too."

"Shut up," said Cirrus, "you just mad cause she made you finally clean your room –"

"That's cause it smelled like socks from hell," said Calypso as she sat down to eat.

"Those are my lucky dancing socks," said Othello. "I don't wash 'em cause they never let me miss a step."

"Anyway," said Neptune, with an eye roll, "I can't wait for talent night, Calypso said your poems are pretty good, Sapphire."

"You know about my poems?" Sapphire asked as he looked at Calypso.

"Being a psychic lets her receive random divine information," said Leonidas.

"Yeah and it sucks, especially when you can't hide weed in your room," said Cirrus.

"You know I don't allow drugs in this apartment," said Leonidas. "Go over to Machiavelli's...or Alexandrite, to do that stuff."

Sapphire thought Leonidas's statement was perplexed. He gave drug dealers protection but he wouldn't allow their merchandise in his own apartment.

"I use my crystal ball to help direct my gift...to use it more clearly," said Calypso. "But that thing is hard to harness, you'd have to practice for years before you could master it like the great Madam Celeste, in Louisiana, my grandmother. Now she's a wonder."

"Oh my gosh, here we go again," said Cirrus.

"Oh, Madam Celeste is so brilliant so powerful,"

mocked Othello.

"Shut up guys," said Calypso.

"I've heard many stories of her when I was a child," said Neptune in her best Calypso impression. "She could read the stars at just six and predict the weather on Mars at eight."

Calypso raised her hand and Othello, Neptune and Cirus' French toast rose up to collide with their faces then fell back on their plates. Napoleon laughed hard as he watched the three mockers syrupy faces.

This made Sapphire chuckle. He felt like family here already. He felt comfortable.

"Hey, guys, please," said Leonidas. "We have a new addition to this family let's not show him how much we're like buffoons just yet."

"Sorry, your highness," whispered Neptune in a childlike manner.

This was a family he could get used to. This was something special that he wanted to be a part of. His family back home was torn in half and his life with Seraphina was no more; this family could be his chance at happiness again.

"Alright, now that everyone is here, let's start with the open discussion," said Leonidas as Sapphire examined his clothing. He was no longer wearing his mother's fur coat; instead, it hung over the chair that he sat in. Today, he wore a crimson vest with an ashy black collar and his signature necklace. "Now, who's going first?"

"Me," Neptune said, her Bob looking shabby to Sapphire, who wondered if it was an intentional style. "I want to share...."

"Alright, let's hear it," said Napoleon.

"Well...I found me a job," said Neptune with a

wide grin.

"Oh, that's great," everyone said simultaneously as if no one wanted to be quiet during her good news. She seemed overjoyed, even Sapphire smiled from what he heard as Calypso served him French toast and slid eggs on his plate.

"It's at this cleaners," said Neptune. "And I know it doesn't pay a lot but it's a start. I mean, I've been unemployed for a whole year!"

"Right," whispered Leonidas.

"And I mean, Leo, you have taken great care of me – you and Calypso. But...but one day I want a home...with a picket fence and a dog and a man and maybe children...."

"Of course," said Leonidas.

"The American dream," said Napoleon.

"And yeah...that's it, that's all I have to say," said Neptune as she played around with her breakfast.

"Okay," said Leonidas.

"Um...I'll go next," said Napoleon. "Um...um...I talked to my ex-wife the other night."

"Good...good," said Leonidas.

"Uh...we ain't talked in so long," said Napoleon. "I really hated her...but I called her and she picked up and...I don't know I was watching this show the other week...it was a segment on forgiveness...."

"Take your time," said Leonidas as Napoleon toyed with the fringe on his black leather jacket. He didn't speak until Leonidas started to grip his shoulder with his ring-adorned fingers.

"Uh," Napoleon said, sliding his blond hair behind his ear, "I learned from the segment that you have to forgive a person for the wrong they did to you...for the hurt...because if you don't...It'll eat you from the inside out. (Leonidas shook his head in agreement). The reason I quit smoking, and I'm glad I did, but the reason I quit was for my girl."

Everyone respected Napoleons time, the floor was his and their eyes became his audience.

"I quit smoking. I did it for her. She said she hated my smell when I came home; I worked as a bartender and had about three smoke breaks a day. I used to smoke way more before her, but I smoked like a train, half a pack a day. Learned from my Daddy, how to do that. But my girl, she'd say, don't smoke around me, so I stopped.

"Then, she said don't smoke anymore, so I told her I'd stop but I didn't. I hid under our basement steps to get a smoke, she caught me of course. I'd smoke and blow out the bathroom window like she couldn't smell it, that was dumb. But she came to me crying on our second anniversary and said she wasn't gonna have a cancer patient for a husband, or an old man carrying around an oxygen tank. Her tears made me stop.

"I knew she lost her mom to smoking or lung cancer, either way, it hurt her to see me do it. So I tried one cigarette a day, but she wasn't happy with that, no so I stopped for a week. The cravings came, ah man, I sat up on our bed one night crying, crying like a baby, cause I just wanted a smoke, man. I would go buy a pack and then dump it in the toilet the next minute. I...would chew...chew anything, gum, candy, peppermints, I started losing sleep over the fact that I couldn't smoke anymore, obsession for that white and red box...obsession for...for a puff.

"I would look in my mirror and notice my face clear up, my breathing felt better. I kept motivating myself to do it for her. Do it for her, man. A month later I had finally stopped for a full three weeks straight without giving in. But it was no use in having my girl replace that void in my heart cause she came out to me that she had gotten pregnant by her boss."

These words clinched Sapphire's heart.

Another victim of cheating.

Another man wounded by the woman he thought loved him.

But he seemed to have an antidote: forgiveness. But Sapphire wasn't ready to forgive anyone, not at all. He wondered if his mother would ever forgive his father, convincing himself that divorce was a sign that she wanted to forget him even more than forgive.

"So, I forgave her, because she might have hurt me...but I'm hurting myself by not forgiving her. That's all I've got to say – oh and the smashing my guitar upstairs is really helping me deal with my anger too, I appreciate that rejuvenation spell you taught me, Leonidas."

"No problem," Leonidas said as he folded his hands.

Napoleon was burning his guitar last night to help with his anger, thought Sapphire. But he had been looked down upon for breaking objects as a way of therapy. Here Napoleon was mutilating his guitar to help ease his anger that he held inside. Sapphire wanted this, he wanted to break a guitar and maybe even set one on fire.

"Well, I can finally say that I don't cry on my Mama's birthday no more like I used to," said Leonidas. "Let's just say I finally healed from her passing...."

"Okay," said Neptune, her eyes deep on Leonidas.

"Alright, now over to Cirrus," said Leonidas. "Whatcha' got?"

"Pass," said Cirrus.

"Oh, no, come on," said Calypso.

"Cirrus, just say something," said Neptune.

"I don't have anything to talk about," said Cirrus with an eye roll. "I'm good, B, there. I'm living my life. Back off."

"Don't pressure him," advised Leonidas.

"Well, I'll go," said Othello. "I tried to get this job at this clothing store and they gave it to the three white dudes that was at the group interview with me. I never got a callback and I'm mad tight, son. I asked why I didn't get the job, right, and they said they wanted someone clean cut with a professional edge –"

"And no braids or black skin," said Calypso.

"Exactly," said Leonidas, "it's bad enough that the pigs ride our back...then all the jobs are all owned by the white devils. Us black men just can't make it."

"Us black men?" said Neptune with a smirk.

"You heard me, mami," Leonidas said with an eye roll.

"Ugh, here we go," said Napoleon.

"You're not black," Neptune said, "you are mixed –"

"I'm a black man!" barked Leonidas. "I'm black, my father was black and his father was black. Just cause my Mama was Hispanic does not stop me from inheriting (Calypso rolled her eyes) my African roots."

"Just drop it, Neptune" said Napoleon.

"Yeah, you don't wanna get the king stirred up," said Calypso as Leonidas ran his fingers through his curly afro.

"Sorry, Leonidas," said Neptune with a smirk.

"No, it's aight, mami," said Leonidas. "I just get worked up discussing my roots. Black history is a powerful (this time, everyone rolled their eyes) very deep thing for me. Those white devils out there try to put us in there whitewashed, systematic, cookie cutter lifestyle, you know, it gets me so tight, B."

Everyone got sort of quiet when Leonidas had started to talk because he was gripping his fist very strongly as if he was holding back some inner frustration that could bust at any moment.

"But not all white people are white devils though," Neptune said.

"I think I know that," said Leonidas. "I mean no disrespect to you or Napoleon; I just don't like how some CAUCASION people, if you will, try to degrade our black roots and our black heritage as if it's not professional...."

"Y'all done got him going," said Calypso.

"But really, they think it's just ugly," said Cirrus, his eyes looking around for a disagreement. "It's mad true, dog. They think our black woman, our children are all ugly, just cause we don't wanna conform to their way of looking."

Sapphire wondered if this was a normal thing here, it made him laugh inside to see the hostility on Leonidas' face. He seemed as if he was a very jolly, very optimistic person until black rights rose up in the conversation.

"Well, let's change the subject," said Napoleon. "Sapphire hasn't shared yet."

All eyes zoomed in on him. Sapphire had a mouth full of egg and he felt like a hungry hobo after devouring his fourth serving of French toast.

"Yeah, Sapphire," Leonidas said. "Let's hear it. What's on your mind?"

Sapphire finished chewing, and fast, trying to lick the syrup from his lips without looking like a walrus. "Um, well, I've been through a lot. Just like everybody else, you know?"

"Right," said Leonidas.

"I've been hurt really badly, by my dad, who just BETRAYED our family. He cheated on my mom... who was nothing but a good wife...and a mother, and that makes me mad cause she stayed in our home all her life to help keep things up, you know? She was married young, ha, younger than I am now. Then shortly after, I found that out, I discovered that – that my own girl cheated on me...."

"That's messed up," said Othello.

Leonidas looked at the front window up the steps, the clouds were beginning to come together in a very gloomy way.

"You know, it's just terrible how you could do a person like that," Sapphire said as he recognized his voice was becoming very frail, almost as if he was being choked. And then a tear embarrassingly fell from his eye.

"Is it raining out?" Neptune asked. "I didn't hear about any rain in the forecast."

"Go on," said Leonidas as he rested his chin on his fist. He looked as if he was not only listening intensively but he was studying Sapphire's movement.

"I mean, I tried to be everything I could be for my girl," Sapphire said as the rain began to bullet against the window by the upstairs steps. "It's just not FARE how you can cheat on a person and not care...not feel anything...it's JUST NOT FARE!"

As Sapphire slammed his fist on the hardwood table, lighting and thunder erupted outside causing everyone to sit up. This wasn't the average lighting that made children frightened this was a bright flash and a crackle of great power.

He was embarrassed that he had gotten out of character, especially on his first time sitting down with everyone.

The bright morning weather was now overtaken by a slowly churning storm.

Leonidas met eyes with Calypso and then he looked back at Sapphire.

"That's all I have to say, right now," said Sapphire with his eyes down on his plate.

"Well, thank you for your share," said Leonidas as he rubbed his hands together as if trying to keep warm. "Calypso, you feel like sharing?"

"Sure," said Calypso. "Well, I have been keeping a close eye on my mom, from the crystal ball she left me, since I first learned how to use it, and she's doing better now. I don't think she'll ever come back here because she can't face me, but I'm just glad she's okay. She's taking care of herself."

"Wonderful," said Leonidas. "Sounds good, I still worry about her myself."

He stood up and pushed his chair in. "I've got a meeting with the other three leaders about this year's Brethren Gathering, so, I'm gonna head out; but y'all continue to get to know Sapphire, I think he will be a great addition to this family. We'll have our talent night after dinner as usual and I really can't wait for that."

"Yes," said Neptune, with great enthusiasm.

"Oh, and Sapphire, maybe you could show us your

grimoire after we hear a poem from you – if it's still cool," said Leonidas as he walked out of the front door.

"No problem," yelled Sapphire. Leonidas had looked at him differently since he had shared, as if he was meant to be studied. What had he done?

"You have a grimoire?" asked Cirrus as he got up from the table.

"Yeah," said Sapphire.

"Uh, go put that plate in the sink," said Calypso as she watched Cirrus try to leave from the table. "You're maid quit a week ago."

Cirrus waved his hand at his plate and it flew into the kitchen but dashed at a wall."

"Dang it!" he said.

"Watch it," said Calypso. "I told you that levitation is something you need to work. It'll never obey you if you just use it when you're ready. You have to constantly practice it, but you too lazy for that."

"Man, I'll get better, B, I ain't buggin'," said Cirrus as Calypso waved her hands causing the remaining dirty plates to fly into the kitchen sink.

"Hey," said Othello, as he nudged Sapphire's arm, "you wanna come upstairs and hear some of my tapes?"

"Yeah," said Sapphire as he got up to go upstairs with Othello, but before he did he turned to Napoleon. "Hey, Napoleon, I would like to do that guitar crashing thing with you later on if that's cool. I think It'll help me with my anger too."

"Sure, bud," said Napoleon. "Heck, both our ladies put us in the same boat, we both deserve to get our feelings off! Knock on my door when you're ready, I'm probably gonna go ride my motorcycle with Cirrus, for a spell – but when I'm back we can kick it, brother."

And after hearing that, Sapphire watched Othello's dance moves upstairs in his room, while listening to Grand Master Flex. They talked about the celebrity crushes they had, the foods they liked and the movies they couldn't stop watching. Othello was very funny and he made Sapphire forget all about his problems.

After Othello did his show and tell with his clothes, Sapphire taught him a spell to summon tiny orbs of lights and Othello couldn't stop casting it after he had mastered the incantation.

They discussed politics, comic strips, television shows and even the unexpected death of 2Pac, that had had a grave effect on everyone.

After the fun evening with Othello, and a nice heap of Calypso's finger sandwiches for lunch, it was beginning to get dark out and Sapphire and Othello critiqued Cirrus' raps in his room. Cirrus had given Sapphire a watch from his collection and even a pair of dark shades to add to his style. He showed Sapphire his stash of guns and gave Othello a pinch for trying to touch one of them.

"Man, I wanna do that prank we pulled on the pizza man last week, B," said Cirrus as Othello rested across his bed.

"What ?" Othello asked with his eyebrows raised. "Oh, the illusion spell –"

"That's it."

"But that pizza man ain't gone come," said Othello. "Not after what you did, and all other delivery joints are too scared to come to Boon Hood."

"Not Wong Song," said Cirrus. "They deliver to

Machiavelli all the time. But to be honest, I ain't even hungry I just wanna have some fun, my G."

Othello sat up as he looked over at Sapphire, who was leaning against a dresser. "Sapphire, the illusion spell that Leonidas taught us is so dope. Wait til you see what Cirrus is gone do to this delivery dude."

With a smile Sapphire looked over at Cirrus who was placing his order on a telephone in his room. This reminded Sapphire that he had a telephone in his room as well. He wondered why he still hadn't called his mother. He was so happy that he was clouded by the things he had left behind.

After Cirrus had placed his order, the three waited by the second-floor window, by the steps, to watch for a delivery vehicle.

"Look at Crystal," said Cirrus as he pointed to the right at a tall, light-skinned, buff man with a low haircut. He was walking into his apartment building across from where Machiavelli's was. "That dude was showing off the craziest stunts when me, Napoleon and him and his older brother was out riding. Othello, I wish Leonidas let you ride with us, man, you would have seen some slammin' stunts, G."

"Awww, man, don't even tell me," said Othello, waving his hand. "I get so heated when Leonidas preaches to me about motorcycles. When you're out of my apartment then you can wreck your body, blah, blah, blah. I'm almost the same age as y'all and he treats me like a baby"

"He just cares," said Sapphire.

"Yeah, I know," said Othello. "I just want to go riding with Crystal and his brother, Topaz, one time, them dudes is sick."

"He's one of the four leaders of Boon Hood,

right?" Sapphire asked.

"Yeah," said Cirrus. "His dad gave it up to him a while ago."

"He's tough though, Crystal is good at keeping the family business afloat. We'll be going to his apartment next year for the Brethren Gathering – and he knows how to party. Unlike Alexandrite, across from us – she's a vampire with the coldest attitude. Her party was dark and blue light's was all around like a psychedelic rave club."

"Most vampires don't be liking them bright lights bruh," said Cirrus. "But she has a daylight ring, so she can go out in the sun. Calypso made it for her and enchanted it to keep her from being burned up whenever she goes outside."

"So, what all happens at this Brethren Gathering?" asked Sapphire.

"Well, it's like everybody comes – old friends show up – Leonidas gives a big speech, he sits at the feast with the leaders, they talk, we party – get wasted."

"Hmm," said Sapphire.

"Except me," said Othello. "I don't get wasted. I have to stay by Calypso the whole time."

"Oh, oh, here he is," said Cirrus. "Okay, here I go."

As a white delivery car pulled up near the steps of Osiris, Cirrus clasped his hands together as if washing them, and said "Imagingo Akananana."

His eyes looked up to the ceiling and he seemed a little weakened by his spell. Cirrus stayed put with Sapphire and Othello but what seemed to be a clone of himself walked towards the delivery car. The delivery man spoke to the clone of Cirrus while he waved his hands in a circular motion, concentrating on his magic. The clone stuck his hand in to hand the Chinese delivery man his money but his hand fell apart from his wrist and into the seat, causing the driver to squeal.

Sapphire and Othello snickered as Cirrus tried to keep himself from bursting into tears.

"Awww, man, can you give me a hand?" asked the Cirrus clone, as the delivery driver shoved away from him. Suddenly the Cirrus clone lost its head and it tumbled into the seat, as well. "Man, I'm losing my head!"

The delivery driver screamed and spat in his language as he drove off in horror. Sapphire, Othello and Cirrus all collapsed on each other as they began to burst into tears.

He knew he could definitely get used to this. The laughter here was a contagious disease that spread through the halls. Happiness, optimism, hope, all these precious things existed in Boon Hood.

Afterwards he and Othello destroyed guitars with Napoleon, while listening to Nirvana.

This was the first time he could destroy things without being chastised by anyone.

He felt free here. He felt alive.

9 DREADLOCKS

The smashing of guitars wasn't the best part of the day, nor was the bountiful breakfast or the friendship he had quickly formed with Othello. But it was talent night that was.

Everyone met in an empty apartment room on the third floor after Leonidas had been the first to display his art in a room to the left of his, that he called his Royal Painting Room. The walls of the room were splattered with all sorts of wild painting strokes and splashes of what looked like blobs of drippy colors.

Leonidas informed Sapphire that art wasn't finished until it was abandoned and he also bragged about how he visited it every day to add more paint splats whenever he felt overwhelmed or angry with life. Everyone seemed to have an artistic way of turning their pain into art; or at least how to release it through a very unique method.

"Leonidas, this is brilliant," Sapphire said as he examined the surroundings of the paint room "It reflects everything that's going on around the world, you know, all of the chaos and all of the confusion. I love it."

"Thank you," Leonidas said as he smiled at Sapphire.

"Man, Basquiat said something in an interview once that he does an awful painting about a girl whenever he gets mad at her...something like that I can't properly get it. But this...this looks like something he would create if he was mad at a girl, this is cool."

After Leonidas demonstrated his artistic abilities by wildly dashing at his walls with his wide paint brush (which was almost as interesting as his spats of paint that he squeezed out of his plastic bottles) Sapphire and the rest of the gang all sat around in metal chairs in an empty room across the hall.

Calypso shared a painting of two angels watching a young black girl rest in her bed, and Cirrus performed two of his raps that was just poetry sped up in Sapphire's mind. Othello danced, Neptune sang a beautiful ballad and Napoleon played his favorite songs from Nirvana on his guitar.

There was love in the room; a love that was like a fume with the ability to make one's heart swell; and Sapphire's heart did swell greatly. No one judged each other for any errors they made. Acceptance was given out freely with a side of support and cheering.

"Alright, Sapphire, you're up next," said Leonidas as he looked at him.

"Let's hear this poetry," said Neptune who was slowly levitating herself from her chair, up and down, up and down.

"Oh, okay cool this is just one that I wrote last night I was just playing around though, said Sapphire as he took out a folded piece of paper from his pocket. "It's titled Dreadlocks."

And he read:

"Oh boy, oh boy, oh boy. How the wind sweeps through them with a gentle kiss. The unraveling of stress and weight falling down my shoulders like ropes that remind me of the times when I first felt them touch my neck. Hang time, they call it. Length.

"I've had these strips of history in my head and once, before I was born, my ancestors twisted a prophecy in their sons and daughters hair and encrypted secrets and stories of ancient times in the strands of their locks while singing our ancestral songs.

"My hair is a testimony of liberation. All of you with dreadlocks, how sweet, how great, how grand is it that you chose freedom over opinion. You chose locking gel over fitting in. You chose to grow your beauty rather than cut it to the length that the world desires.

"Oh how fun, oh how enjoyable it is to see the curls, braids, plaits, crinkles, colors, textures, strands, shapes, lengths and time spans of the mighty dreadlocks. You inspire a nation. You inspire a world to own their own crown, grow their own crown, style their own crown, become their own crown. I tell you this: a dreaded head is truly a crowned head, and don't you ever forget it."

Everyone seemed so caught up in his reading while he pronounced each word with care. When he had finished they all seemed astounded as if they had never heard any poem that good.

"That was mad wicked, dude," said Cirrus.

"Bravo, bravo," said Calypso. "I've got to get that from you and hang it up on my wall, Sapphire."

"Oh really, thanks, but the really good ones are in

my painting room. I'll get em, hold on guys."

Sapphire visualized his painting room, and suddenly he was there

He had done it without almost having to put any effort into it. And he didn't feel weak at all; it was as if he had gotten a rush of energy instead.

Sapphire looked around at all of the paintings, all of the words he had magically placed over his walls.

His painting room.

Could he leave it behind? He had done things in this room that he cherished, all the paintings and the writing; but he had done a horrible deed as well and he wanted to forget that.

Coming back here was a different experience than before, a sad experience. He wanted to go back to his new place of refuge. He wanted to be back with his new family.

And so he grabbed his backpack, stuffed it with his grimoire, two pairs of jeans he had laying around and a few pins and blank paper. He wondered if he tried to teleport again would he get lost like before. He couldn't leave Osiris for too long, he had to be back.

He took one last look at his paintings, swearing within himself to return for a visit and then closed his eyes to once again be in the company of his new friends.

In an instant, he vanished in a puff of black smoke. Once back in the company of everyone he noticed that they were all standing around him in a circle, smiles on everyone's faces. Leonidas had Nekita around his neck and looked very proud, Sapphire didn't know what was going on, but due to all the other weird things that had happened around here he didn't read too deep in it.

"What's everybody looking at?" Sapphire asked.

"Wow," whispered Calypso as she smiled at Sapphire.

"How do...how do you feel?" Leonidas asked as he looked at him.

"I feel, I feel fine," said Sapphire.

Everyone looked as if they had been told a secret, or at least was ready to give out one.

"You don't feel tired?" Leonidas asked.

"Nope," said Sapphire, "just a little hungry – I could use some more of Calypso's French toast, ha ha...."

"Take Nekita," said Leonidas, "give her a command, tell her to do something – go ahead."

Leonidas placed his snake over Sapphire's neck (causing him to slightly cringe) and looked very excited while doing so. "Tell her to do something, man."

Sapphire cringed as Nekita rested on his shoulder. "Why?" he asked.

"Just do it," said Cirrus. "Come on, we've got to know."

"Um," said Sapphire, "Nekita, coil around my right arm – softly. I can't lose my good writing arm, girl."

Humbly, she obeyed Sapphire's words, coiling herself around Sapphire's arm very gently.

"I never thought I'd live to see one again," Leonidas said. "The signs of a superior spell caster are of the three: the ability to manipulate weather – like calling lightning from the sky or – a tornado or rain. The second sign is great magical endurance; long-lasting energy when using powerful spells. And the

92

third is dominion over all creatures. Sapphire, my brotha', you are a...a superior spell caster."

10 MOJO

Hearing that he was one of the most powerful beings in Boon Hood was good news, but hearing that his mother was doing fine in her home was even better. The morning after finding out about his great power, Sapphire called his mother and hearing her voice made everything feel as if it were alright now.

His father had left home to go live at a hotel and she had been encouraged and strengthened by Aunt Rene. Sapphire had told her that he had found refuge at an apartment for sorcerers but did not include that it was in a drug infested neighborhood.

He didn't tell her the real reason why he left Seraphina's home but informed her that they were not getting along because of petty disagreements. He wanted to be sensitive about his mother's condition, her divorce to come, her aching heart. Now was not the time to bombard her with Seraphina's cheating.

Leonidas had begged Sapphire to act as a teacher for everyone in the apartment on Tuesdays and Thursdays, and although he didn't think himself worthy because he had just received his power the night before, he didn't deny the opportunity to give back to the community that had given so much to him.

On Wednesday, in the kitchen, the voodoo king

displayed his own magic in front of everyone. Leonidas, with his hands rubbing together, stood over a voodoo doll that had been enchanted with a strand of Calypso's hair. "By the power of my ancestors," he said, as he stretched out his arms and then clasped them back together.

Calypso seemed to be linked with the doll now, as she would move her arm every time Leonidas would move one of the dolls plushy limbs.

"Lay off, you had your fun, dude," said Calypso, with a huff.

"Ancestral magic takes time to learn, Sapphire," said Leonidas as he released his spell from the voodoo doll. "It's the ancient practice of using the magic that exists within your bloodline...your lineage for strength...for powerful spells."

Leonidas put wonder in Sapphire's heart. He spoke to him about voodoo with a serious tone, as if warning him of something very dangerous.

"It's fantastic," said Sapphire.

"But I'm just controlling her body...with this doll," said Leonidas. He looked around at everyone and his eyes widened. "There is an ancient voodoo spell to control the mind."

"Really?" Sapphire asked in a faint breath.

"Really."

"What's the incantation?"

Leonidas looked at Sapphire and then over at Cirrus. "Zomb Zing Zo," he said as he looked into Cirrus's brown eyes that became a glossy white, while his mouth hung open lazily.

Everyone observed Cirrus very closely, he didn't move, but made a loud, "gaaaaahhhh," sound from his wide opened mouth.

"Do the creep," said Leonidas.

Cirrus started to dance; his eyes still white, his mouth still opened wide.

"The things that I command him to do are now his life's goals," said Leonidas as Cirrus danced, causing everyone to burst into giggles. "He wants to please me…he wants to do everything I tell him to do. This is where the idea of Zombies that are used in pop culture came from, Sapphire. His brain is mine, his will is mine, but only after I look him in his eye's which are –"

"The windows of the soul," said Calypso, smiling with her purple colored lips. "No one has been able to master this spell but the king, Sapphire. But since you're a superior now you could do it – I bet."

"Oh, I don't know," said Sapphire as Leonidas wrote his incantation on a sticky note and gave it to Sapphire.

"I bet you could master it the first time," said Leonidas as he looked at Cirrus and said, "I release you," and he returned to his normal self.

To Sapphire, voodoo seemed too complex to grasp. He had cast more advanced spells from his grimoire this week than ever before but wasn't sure if he was ready for Leonidas's traditional magic.

Later that night, Sapphire had relaxed in Othello's room. After being plagued with boredom he asked Othello if he wanted to learn a new spell. A transformation spell.

Othello sprung up from his bed and sat with Sapphire, eager to learn a new incantation.

"Say it with me," said Sapphire as he traced his

hand over his spell books tan page.

Together the two said, "Metramorpha Tora."

Sapphire picked up an old apple that was on Othello's nightstand and said his incantation and it became a black cat in his hands.

"Whoa," said Othello as he gazed at Sapphire's transformation.

"Here, hold her," Sapphire said as he gave the black cat over to Othello. "She's cute, huh, and she's the real thing. Think about what you want the object to transform into, desire it as you cast your spell. It takes focus...practice. Right the spell down and practice it. But be careful not to try and transform anything living into another thing, that takes greater skill...much more practice."

Just then, Leonidas had entered into the room.

"Hey, Othello, I'm going to see Selene, you two wanna come?"

"Yeah, I'm down," said Othello as he jumped up to put on his shoes.

Sapphire was happy to be invited to go out with them, it felt good to be in the loop. Othello told Sapphire that Leonidas was going to buy hamburgers, a tradition he created whenever he would take him out with him.

After stuffing their faces with burgers, they rode in Leonidas's black Cadillac to an apartment building that was merged next to a video store. The entire ride was full of Leonidas playing old tapes from the 70s and repeatedly asking the boys, "what y'all youngsters know about this?"

This was Sapphire's fourth day in Boon Hood and he guessed that Leonidas invited him on this trip to get to know him more or maybe for him to get to know Leonidas more. Either way, he felt like family because of this invitation.

Leonidas turned to Sapphire who sat in the front as he parked his car. "Selene, my cousin, works as a photographer here in this apartment. She lives on the top floor. This is my mom's side of the family."

"Selene is so hot," said Othello as he got out of his side to stretch his legs.

"She needs a favor from me," said Leonidas. "Everybody calls on the voodoo man when they need a favor."

"A favor?" said Sapphire.

"Yup, a little magic to help them along the way," said Leonidas.

Together the three walked in the apartment that had its first floor turned into some open photography room with rusted tile floor, black curtains and weird people, who were dressed weird while doing weird dances.

Sapphire had really been introduced to a different Side in New York since being in the company of Leonidas. Not only did some of the people wear questionable things in Boon Hood but in the night, the freaks came out and the freaks all seemed to come here in black ripped leather, oversized clothing, piercings, tattoos of a plenty and wild hair.

Fashion had taken over New York and high fashion was its predecessor.

Sapphire guessed that Leonidas must have taken his colorful way of dressing from this side of the family.

98

"That's Selene," said Othello as he pointed to the woman in the center of the room who was dancing to the boom box while snapping photos of a black man on a stool with roses in his dreadlocks and paint all over his body.

Because he was an artist, this excited Sapphire as he found several meanings for this pose.

Selene had on a black mini dress, choosing to dress lighter than her company, and her slick hair was kept in a ponytail down her back.

"Aye, look who's here," she said as she stopped taking shots and rushed to hug Leonidas. "How are you, Papi?"

"Good, good, Ay, dios mio," said Leonidas as Selene kissed his cheeks like a mother would. Sapphire guessed she was the older cousin.

Everyone looked excited to see the king come in, but Selene looked as if a hero had returned home. She conversed with him, slipping in and out of English and Spanish as she waved her hands. Sapphire always thought it was funny when people talked with their hands.

They walked upstairs and down a hall that led to a room where an ashy fireplace was. Two chairs were inside, fancy ones and Othello and Sapphire sat in them while Selene retrieved something for Leonidas.

The mantle on the fireplace had a picture of Leonidas's mother and he kissed it before lighting a candle next to it.

"I'm making a gris gris bag for my cousin," said Leonidas as he turned to Sapphire. "It's a type of mojo that grants the owner fortune…or misfortune, depending on what kind of spell I perform. It's old,

old magic. Of the rarest kind passed down from my pops."

"I've heard of a gris gris bag," said Sapphire. "They originated in Africa."

"That's right," said Leonidas.

"The motha' land," said Othello as he noticed Selene return.

She entered in with something in her hand; it appeared to be boxer briefs, gray ones. Sapphire sank in his armchair as Selene walked up to Leonidas.

"Here's what you wanted, cousin," Selene said. "A bit of his DNA, in his boxer he left…and a little DNA in this comb. Will this work?"

"Yeah," said Leonidas as he took the two things from Selene. "This will work."

Selene turned to Sapphire who was joking to Othello about Leonidas holding another man's underwear.

"I know you've felt it too," she said as Sapphire sat up.

He looked confused at her as she played with her red fingernails. Then she looked him in his eyes.

"I have empathy, a blessing from my mother, she gave us kids the ability to feel others emotions as our own, because that was something my father could never do, or never wanted to do. But…I know how you feel…how it feels to be cheated on. You think you've got something good, and that what you have is unbreakable and that no girl or boy can get between it. It feels like failure. You say to yourself 'am I worthy of love at all'? Am I worthy of a relationship? I mean at first you meet a good person, like my guy — he's sweet, or at least he was.

"You start to feel like you've got something good, like – like what he is is a...good thing. He treats you real good, takes you out, and buys you nice stuff."

No one dared interrupted Selene as she spoke. The happy photographer from downstairs was now a gloomy patient and the boys were the shrinks.

"He does all the things a good person should do. At times you're not even sure if you deserve it. He meets your mother and your brother...you know your whole family and then you talk about getting serious...you know...actually making plans to marry.

"Together...you talk about what ya' gonna name your kids, the real mushy stuff. You take out a loan to one day buy a house, nothing too big just something to fit you him and his child in, maybe. He tells you things like that you're not fat, your're just full in all the right places – and that you have the most beautiful laugh and that your skin is his favorite texture. He actually said that, ha. He actually said that. But then, just when you think its solid you walk into your bedroom one day and there he is laying with another woman.

"Then, you feel ugly, not good enough. You feel a burning in your stomach like – I don't know bad take out or something – you know how that stuff feels, its sick. Yeah, that's how it feels. That's how it feels to be cheated on."

As if to break the tight tension that had formed in the air, Leonidas said, "alright, so this'll only take a minute and then your boyfriend will be eating out the palm of your hand."

Sapphire wanted to digest Selene's words but was caught off guard by Leonidas who was about to create a gris gris bag and he had never seen one created before.

Leonidas took the comb and the boxer briefs and placed them inside his pouch. He pulled the drawstring and cast the bag down to the floor. He then opened his arms and said an Incantation too soft for Sapphire to hear. He repeated his words over and over in a faint whisper and fell to his knees as his eyes squinted. His back was turned to everyone but they knew he was in discomfort because of his grunting.

Othello didn't look amused but Sapphire sat up in his seat, legs curled under him as Selene leaned against the wall.

What shocked Sapphire the most about this whole ordeal was the ghostly figures that crawled up the walls looking as if they were shadows of beast from another world. Maybe another planet? They had green frames and they glowed, their images were similar to human shadows.

Sapphire looked over to the others, but they were not moved at all, only he was in awe. The figures slid up to the ceiling and shot straight into the bag that had opened itself for them to dive in. Once they were inside, Leonidas drew the strong again and sealed it.

"It is done," he said as he stood up, struggling to stand.

"Thank you, thank you so much," said Selene as she forceful slid money into Leonidas's pocket. "Take the money, Leo, come on. And thank you, again, I really appreciate you coming here. And this is full proof, huh?"

"Yup," said Leonidas. "He won't want no woman but you – he won't love you, though, Selene. This doesn't create love, this bag just draws you all together forever – you're not going to be able to get rid of him. Unless –"

"Unless?" said Selene.

"Unless you burn this bag to crisp, the mojo will continue on until he is dead."

The city lights buzzed through the mist that the rain brought. Sapphire sat in the back of the Cadillac as Othello sat up front by Leonidas. Othello had fallen asleep as soon as they had left Selene's home but Sapphire sat up straight, eyeing the view of brownstone apartment buildings, it reminded him of his home.

His mind was taken to the halls he ran through with his father, the kitchen he ate his mother's meals in – and now was that all over?

Did he ever want to go back home? They had lived in that place since his birth and he had not known another home, until now, until Leonidas.

Selene's words were in his head bouncing around. He was angry that she had reminded him of the pain he had tried to forget. Selene had been stung by the same feeling; didn't she know that it was a feeling that should be forgotten?

"You alright?" said Leonidas as he looked at Sapphire from his review mirror.

"Yeah, I'm coo'," Sapphire said.

"I know it hurts, I ain't ever been cheated on, but I mean I know its wack – but I just want you to know you can always talk to me about it."

"Thank you," said Sapphire as he held onto his hands. He used to do that with Seraphina, he would grip a hold of her hands but now he had his one to grip, he was gonna try it on his own for a long time.

No more dates for at least a year, he told himself. That would help the healing.

"I think it's crazy that all this happened, Leonidas."

"What do you mean?"

"My mom finds out her husband is a cheater…and then her own child finds out the same just hours later, a lot of people wouldn't believe me if I told them. Ha, I just still can't believe it. My mom was good...she was a good lady, just like I know I was a good man. I'm only, twenty, I know, but I can offer any woman loyalty – honesty and passion...."

He stopped as Leonidas turned a corner; they were getting close to Boon Hood.

"I'm sorry about your parents," said Leonidas. "I loved my mom and pop, they were my all…they argued but they never split. It would have hurt me, too, if they had…divorce is a very emotional strain; especially if what they had was…worth staying for."

Outside were homeless people caught up in the rain. They stood on bus stops, under trees and on the steps of abandoned buildings, anywhere they could get shelter. They all stood still, giving Sapphire the impression that they were frozen in time. His mind always wondered off on things, it was the artist in him. To Sapphire, these loiterers were all apart of some play on the street and they were standing still, the old man in a torn coat, the couple on the steps hunched together and the two women under the tree with bags, were all actors getting ready for a theatrical performance. Music would start and they would burst out in song about how hard it was to live in the poverty soaked streets of New York.

"Time heals all wounds," said Leonidas as he awoke Sapphire from the play he was directing in his head.

The tires of the car became slick on the street that was beginning to fill up with rainwater. Sapphire rolled up his window as to avoid getting wet. A tear fell down his face and he leaned his head against the glass.

"You'll be alright, my brother," said Leonidas. "It'll get better."

11 Creature

The lessons that Sapphire taught were scheduled after lunch on Tuesdays and Thursdays. In the painting room, they all practiced levitation together on a small flower pot.

One by one they each worked their magic; floating the pot while concentrating like Sapphire had instructed.

Cirrus was good at levitation just like Calypso and Leonidas, but that didn't stop them from joining in the lesson.

He taught them with spoons, and they each held one together as they bent them backward and forwards. Calypso was the best at it, as she would make everyone's spoon wrap around their fingers.

"No fair, show off," grumbled Neptune.

Next, they levitated each other, focusing on not dropping their partner.

Leonidas hovered himself in the air, floating above everyone else. He too was good at this form of magic. Moving matter without hands. The spiritual level Leonidas was on did not make much sense to Sapphire. He couldn't fathom the idea of ancestral power. He didn't understand.

Leonidas landed down on his feet and stretched his arms out.

"Can you explain voodoo to me?" Sapphire asked as he heard a loud bump. In the corner, Cirrus had just dropped Othello after not being able to hold him up for long.

"You alright," said Leonidas.

"Don't laugh," said Calypso as she turned to see Cirrus cackling. "You're not gonna want us to laugh at you when you trip down the stairs tomorrow."

"No I won't," said Cirrus. "You just playing."

"No, I'm not, my visions see the inevitable. You're gonna fall down the whole flight."

Leonidas held his stomach in laughter as he walked to Sapphire. "You wanna know about voodoo?"

"Yeah, sure, I still don't understand how it works. I know you've been trying to get me to understand it, but it's just so mysterious." Sapphire said.

"I feel like I'm making a trade with a pilgrim like my ancestors did in their day. You bring over to my kingdom a book of foreign spells in exchange for the secrets to voodoo."

"Everybody, get ready for another history lesson," said Calypso as she gathered her lime green dress and sat down on the floor.

"It all began," Leonidas said as he snapped his fingers and summoned a puff of purple smoke that filled the room, "in Nigeria, many years ago."

The purple fumes that Leonidas summoned had been inhaled by everyone and it seemed to have them envision whatever Leonidas wanted them to see. They were no longer in the apartment anymore but in a village where an African Shaman stood around a group of tribesmen.

"What was that stuff? Sapphire wondered. He not only was in another world but he could hear all of the things that went on around him. Sounds like, drum beating, crackling fire and tribal chants from the Shaman could be heard.

"Relax," said Calypso as she put her hand on Sapphire's shoulders. "It's just Ala dust, Leonidas can put visions in your mind very easily, when you inhale it. It's harmless, only temporary."

"Our Shaman, named Oluko, a friend of my great grandfather, taught our people the ways of channeling our ancestor's power. He studied the waves of energy in the air and discovered that when a magician died their power lived on in the atmosphere. He absorbed that power and used it to make his magic stronger. Many traveled to our tribe to learn our secrets, trading vegetables, fish and cattle, for healing ailments, hexes and strong charms. The Shaman not only could channel more energy but with it he could create more diverse and more powerful spells.

"Together, the Shaman gained wealth with my great grandfather who had won our land and became its new king. The Agbara clan taught many how to use the ancient practice of voodoo to many clans that were captured years later by white slave traders – and this is how voodoo made its way to many American states."

"Wow," Sapphire whispered as the scene changed to a child being healed by an old African woman in a hut. She stood over him with her hands on his chest. While chanting, she watched as the boy awakened from a sleep-like state and then rejoiced.

Leonidas turned to Sapphire and said, "see, you

108

cast your spell's using the strength of your magic alone…that lives in your belly. But voodooist use the power of their ancestors to merge with their own. As you know it, spells take energy, lots of it, so, voodoo allows us to practice powerful magic without losing strength."

"I see," Sapphire said.

The scene changed once more to a young boy, who sat at his father's feet. With bright skin and curly hair, everyone recognized him to be little Leonidas. His father sat at his throne, that sat on the third floor and held onto his war staff. Osiris looked proud as his son summoned small holographic images of animals in the palms of his hands.

Leonidas stretched out his arms. "We have been passing this tradition down for years. Like our pride…it is the beauty of our culture."

Suddenly, the room was back in place, no more Nigeria, tribesmen or Shaman.

"That was beautiful," said Sapphire.

"I'm glad I got to show you a piece of my history," Leonidas said.

Sapphire smiled, "I'm glad I get to experience it."

To teach here felt liberating for him, in fact, this whole new neighborhood was liberating for him. He hadn't thought about Seraphina all day, and as he went along with the course he realized that this new life he had with them was a gift for his sufferings.

Bel Biv Davoe played loudly and so many dance breaks happened while he taught, but he didn't mind the interruptions.

"Trust in your magic," Sapphire said as he stood behind Othello who struggled to make the flower pot

109

rise. "Don't envy anyones…magic, don't compare, don't covet…trust in the gift you have. Believe in yourself. Don't doubt yourself."

Friday was a nice evening, the first snow, that didn't last long, had fallen and they all watched outside while drinking Calypso's hot chocolate.

Saturday, they all relaxed together and roasted marshmallows over the kitchen stove. Leonidas told creepy ghost stories while jumping and making everyone scared and upset.

Sunday, Sapphire and Othello went on another run with Leonidas who had to go visit his cousin, Orion, Selene's younger brother.

Leonidas said that he always liked to travel with his boy, Othello, but he didn't wanna leave Sapphire at the apartment alone to miss out on all the adventures, plus he had formed a liking to Sapphire like he was his older brother.

Monday had come and everyone shared at breakfast.

Leonidas went on telling a story of how he and Calypso first learned how to morph into animals from his father. It was amusing to everyone else to hear about Leonidas getting stuck as a puppy for an hour before his mother discovered it was him, but to Sapphire it was fantastic.

All this magical talk and nobody acted weird about hearing the words spell or enchantment.

He had been coached by his father to never spill his magical talent, and with the exception of Seraphina, he had never gotten to.

"My birthdays Wednesday," said Othello as he devoured his pancakes. "Anybody, uh, you know, planning something like a surprise party for me?"

"If we told you, boy, it wouldn't be a surprise," said Calypso. She looked very dolled up today with colorful makeup and a turban wrapped around her long braids.

Leonidas took a sip of his orange juice and said, "I didn't even know your birthday was coming up, brotha' man."

"Did too," said Othello.

Leonidas chuckled. "I know, you're gonna be twenty years old. How could I forget my man's b-day?"

"Sho' is," said Othello. "Me and Sapphire gone finally be the same age. Aye, Leonidas, can I get a pet snake like yours for my birthday?"

"Nope!"

"Ah, come on."

"Nope. I said no, Othello. You can't take care of a snake."

"But I'm bout to be twenty—"

"I don't care, chico," said Leonidas.

"What would you do with a snake, anyway?" asked Neptune.

"Feed it mice, talk to it, sleep with it," said Othello, "walk around with it on my neck like Leonidas."

"Nope," said Calypso. "Cause you'd probably let it out to scare me, knowing you."

Neptune cackled. "That sounds like him."

111

After breakfast and a big lunch, Sapphire sat up in Othello's room while they discussed what they were gonna do for talent night.

To have a platform to express his talent for writing was good for him.

Cirrus had come into the room to perform his rap for tonight and did it over and over until Sapphire felt sick.

"Can't believe my birthdays almost here," said Othello.

"Ah, yeah, you turning three?" said Cirrus.

"Shut up, bro," said Othello as Sapphire snickered.

The teasing from Cirrus was hilarious, he knew how to push Othello's buttons in the smallest of ways.

Later that night, after Cirrus's rap, an emotional singing selection from Neptune and Othello's break dancing, Sapphire read his poem.

Nervously, he stood up, Leonidas made him stand. He was so proud to hear his 'brotha" perform that he sat on the edge of his seat to hear.

"This piece is called This House. Well, here it goes."

And he read:

"This House. With a foundation built on ancestry, and floor boards of wood polished with harmony this house is here for artistry this house was built to inspire. It opens its shutter's and through glass

112

windows shines the sun that blazes straight inside. This house was built and inside is a fire this house was built to aspire. Its roof is covered in long stringy hair, nappy happy dreaded hair; inside its attic is treasure's there, this house was built to always share.

"its family is its beams and holds like the nails in between, this house is full of old history, this house was built for peace. This house is firm and it stands proudly in the day. It opens its door to speak truth loud and proud. No one can shut it, for who can deny that what it's saying? Who can stop its chimney from releasing its steam, especially after a long day of work?

"Who can stop this house from dropping rotting shingles from its sides that no longer serve a purpose, who can? This house was built for a mother to feed her baby in, for a father to read a bedtime story to his children in, for a grandma to hang her pretty new curtains, in for sisters to talk about that new hot boy down the street in, for grandpa to say, "stop that racket in here," in, this house was built for love.

"In the night, flashes of lightning whip and lash at this house like the whips the old slave master hit his people with and it hurts. This house has seen hurt. This house has felt pain and it has cried many nights. This house wanted to burn down to the ground and be done with this cruel retched world where crows gnaw at its frame and wasp hide under its siding, where bad children and adults that act like children kick at its door, this house, yes this house was built to endure.

"This house has a dark and scary past but it perseveres like ain't nothing happened or ever has this house goes on like a train on its tracks this house was built to last. Come in, come in all you children, to play and to run. Bring your dolls, jump ropes and toy guns. Come in, come in you won't be shunned for this house, yes this house was built for fun. Come in and play music loud, on old record players and speakers if you have a chance, this house was made to sing and Dance.

"Come and enjoy yourself but come fast, for the living room is swelling. This house was made for dwelling. This house was made for dwelling, this house was made for dwelling."

As usual, the applause came along with many head swelling compliments.

Calypso looked just as proud as Leonidas was, "you're inspiring me to write, now," she said.

"How come my words never inspired you to rap then, Calypso?" asked Cirrus as he was nudged by Neptune.

"Shut up, fool," said Calypso. "And all your raps call women out their names and you use nigga in every sentence –"

"Hey, now, this is a judge free zone," said Leonidas, with his hands up.

"Any way," said Calypso, "I'm ready to hear Napoleon play–"

She stopped. Calypso stopped talking and then turned to Othello. "What did you do?" she asked as she eyed Othello down. "You created something? I just got a vision of something…horrible…ugly. It's downstairs!"

CAAAAAAWWWW! Something downstairs had just made an eerie sound, something like a loud crow, maybe a person was making the sound? It made Leonidas jump up.

"Summon the war staff," said Calypso as she stood up by Leonidas. "This thing is ravenous."

"What is it, Calypso?" he asked as an emerald staff with a red gem at its tip appeared out of green smoke and into his hand.

"Othello created something and he hid it in the storage downstairs," said Calypso as she pinched Othello in his arm.

"Ouch, man, why you gotta' beat up on me?" asked Othello. "He's not bad, I just wanted a snake-like Leonidas so I tried to turn a crow I caught outside into one...but he look like...um...not like a snake. He's not dangerous, he's the size of my arm."

"Well, he grew!" said Calypso as she walked out to the hall and clasped her mouth. "Leonidas...come quick."

Everyone followed out with Leonidas and stood in awe as what looked like a black crow with dark feathers, a dark, leathery body, and snake-like eyes the size of apples and a yellow beak stood at the very end of the hall.

"You used the spell on something living?" asked Sapphire as he turned to Othello. "I told you not too. Your power is not strong enough for living transformations yet."

"Is it...evil?" asked Neptune as she hid behind Calypso.

The creature began to walk closer with its crow like claws for feet, but it moved slow as if it was scared or maybe sizing up the magicians.

"I can hear his thoughts?" said Calypso. "That's very rare...I usually can't tell what people are thinking, but...it's half snake, half crow. Part of his brain wants worms...the other part wants us for its meal."

"That thang ain't eatin' me," said Napoleon, "I'm getting my shotgun!"

When Napoleon ran, using the staircase behind them, it seemed to trigger the half crow, half snake humanoid. It flew with its wide wings, that swept at the walls, and aimed for Sapphire. It had teeth like a viper and that made Sapphire's stomach weak.

Leonidas shoved Sapphire out of the way and swung at the creature with his staff, giving its beak a whack!

The creature flew backward as it hovered away down the stairs.

"It's coming for Napoleon!" said Calypso as Leonidas followed after the creature.

"Split up!" said Leonidas as he ran. "Trap 'em!"

Sapphire and Othello ran towards Leonidas's direction as Calypso, Cirrus and Neptune went the other way down the stairs. Now everyone was on the second floor. Napoleon came out of his room with his gun and shot at the creature but missed his core parts, only grazing the left wing.

Calypso tried to run in her long dress that swept her feet; she stood in front of Napoleon and caused the creature to smash into the ceiling on the second floor and then dash into the red carpet.

Leonidas shot a bolt of green light from his war staff and it seemed to make the creature angry as it screeched. Steam sprung from a wound in its rib side.

"Poor thing is hurt," said Neptune.

"You feelin' sorry for this thing?!" said Cirrus. "He tried to eat Napoleon!"

"We need to bind it!" said Sapphire. "Hold it so I can disentangle him."

"Everyone, arms out!" said Calypso as she held the creature in a telekinetic bind. Everyone held their hands out as the creature tried to fight their power but when they worked together against him he could not prevail.

"Hold him!" said Sapphire.

The creature floated in midair with loud disapproval of being held captive.

Sapphire had learned a spell from his mother to unbind a person from a magical jinx or an enchantment mishap. He wasn't afraid to approach the winged creature with snake eyes and sharp teeth. He was a superior spell caster and he wanted to act like it. He had strong power and wanted to exemplify it.

"Lower him down," he said, and everyone followed his instructions. "Alright, big boy, time to bring you down to size," he said as he waved his hands over the creatures frame, "Vinculis Amittere Solvitum," he said repeatedly as the creature morphed into a normal sized black crow with a broken wing fluttering around on the floor.

"Aw, it's so cute," said Neptune. As she perched down to nestle the bird in her bosom. "Leonidas, can I keep him?"

"No, he might have rabies," said Leonidas. "Sapphire, heal its wing and send him off?"

"Absolutely," said Sapphire as he healed the crow that struggled to be free from Neptune.

"I can't believe you're touching it," said Calypso.

"Aw, I've always wanted a little birdy for a pet," said Neptune. "My parents wouldn't let me have anything after I deliberately killed all our goldfish."

"Whoa, what?" said Leonidas.

"Time to go," said Sapphire as he pointed his finger at the crow and cast him into the night sky above.

"Very good work everybody. We're so much stronger when we work together as a team," said Leonidas. "But you," he said as he looked at Othello, "I don't want you trying to morph anything else, got that!"

"Yeah, man, I got it," said Othello as Sapphire looked over at him in disbelief.

"You're going to have to wait until you're old enough to get your own place to have your own pet snake," said Leonidas. "My home...my rules. Nekita is thoroughly watched by me, and I make sure that she's tended to all the time. You're not ready for that responsibility. Now I don't know about y'all, but this night has drained me completely, I'm going to bed before something else tries to eat us."

"Me too," said Cirrus.

"Me three," Calypso added.

"Hey, Sapphire," said Othello as he walked up towards Sapphire. "I'm sorry, man, that I didn't listen. I just wanted a pet snake so bad."

"It's cool, dude," said Sapphire. "I ain't mad. Let's just go to sleep."

"Can I crash in your room tonight," said Othello.

"Let me guess, you scared to sleep alone tonight?"

"Nah, bro bro. Okay, yes, yes I am."

"Come on, crash on my floor, dude."

12 JUBILATION

It was Wednesday morning. Sapphire awoke to the smell of pancakes as he stretched out in an orange sweater he had retrieved from Othello's room.

He peeked out his window to see that there were no snowflake's falling from a gloomy sky. It was warmer today and that was surprising for New York weather.

Sapphire turned behind him as he heard Othello banging on everybody's door, proclaiming that today was his birthday. Sapphire would have been popped for doing this at his house.

Of course, the generous Sapphire gave Othello a card that he had hand painted and enchanted to change colors. Inside the card was $20 and a heartfelt note. That was classic Sapphire always thinking about others.

Most of the gifts from the others was money. Cirrus had passed down some sneakers and Leonidas and Calypso gave him a new boom box, a camcorder (that Leonidas had more fun with) and new tapes to dance to, from his favorite artist.

Leonidas taped the whole event and did more singing to the camera while listening to Sade, then letting anyone else talk to the camera. Othello unboxed all his gifts with glee, and then, the biggest gift arrived at his door with a knock.

"Uh oh," said Calypso, "is that who I think it is?"

"Who?!" asked Othello as he marched outside to see his mother standing with a red bike with a big white bow on it.

He jumped into her arms and then jumped on the bike. Othello's mother looked just like him just with more height, and a thinner face. She wore a blue windbreaker, crimped, gold earrings and her hair was slicked back into a ponytail.

"Aye, yo', Othello," said some guys outside of Crystals apartment across the street, "that's all you?"

"Yup," said Othello. "It's my birthday."

"Happy birthday, youngin'," one of them said as he puffed from his joint.

Along came Machiavelli, for the party. He was one of the four leaders in Boon Hood. As he walked across the street his dreadlocks slapped at his waist. He had come over from his apartment to give Othello his first drink for his birthday, but Leonidas would not permit it.

"He's too young," said Leonidas as he gave Machiavelli a wink.

"Ah, come on, I can't have no fun!" said Othello as Sapphire laughed at the fact that Leonidas was so overprotective of him.

Harmony, Othello's mother, pulled a sheet cake from her car and they all enjoyed it in the dining hallway.

Every time Othello would blow out his twenty candles, Cirrus and Napoleon would continue to light them, after becoming proficient in fire manipulation from last night's lesson.

Sapphire had gotten everyone into creating fire and changing its shape and size. He couldn't decide which was better, the salary from Leonidas to teach or the chance to help educate magical folk.

Another one of the leaders of Boon Hood came to see Othello, and his name was Crystal. He had bright skin, a muscular frame, and blue eyes. He ate more cake than anyone else and took a portion of Othello's birthday alcohol from Machiavelli.

For a leader, Crystal wasn't as esteemed as Leonidas was. Instead, he joked a lot, and to Sapphire's annoyance, tried to recite a poem for him.

"So, you do poetry?" he asked as he looked at Sapphire.

"He does," Leonidas said with a grin. "Good poetry too."

"Well, let me spit something to you, B," Crystal said.

Oh no, Sapphire thought.

Crystal raised up and said, "I'm so fresh, fresher than clean socks, I run these streets, man, and it don't stop!"

"Oooooh," said Machiavelli as he grinned over at Leonidas.

Whatever else Crystal had said did not reach Sapphire's ears because he stopped listening. His attention shifted over to Othello's mother who couldn't take her eyes off of him. Was she in awe that he had grown up to be such a handsome man, or was she in awe because he had grown up to be a handsome man without her?

Sapphire, in his head, named her a bad mother. How could she show up with gifts and a bike after abandoning her son? And was she still on drugs, was she even clean now?

He didn't like the way she acted as if everything was back to normal but Othello didn't mind it, so Sapphire tried not to feel hard-hearted. He was just happy that Othello was happy.

Sapphire noticed all the similar things that Othello and his mother did. She was nice. He noticed that she had to knock at the apartment door, it wouldn't open for her by itself, which meant she wasn't a magician. He must have gotten his magical bloodline from his father, someone he never spoke about.

After cake, roasting one another and Calypso's double-decker cheeseburgers, the boys sat outside while Leonidas went off with Machiavelli and Crystal. It was said, by Othello, that Alexandrite, the leader of the apartment to the left of theirs, rarely came outside, because the sun didn't please her vampiric eyes. But then again, Othello said she didn't like him anyway, and that was the real reason why she stopped by. Maybe, Sapphire thought, because of his obnoxious sense of humor.

After Othello's mother had gone, four young men, a little older than Sapphire, came down to Boon Hood and asked to ride Othello's bike. The one who was the leader, or at least did all the talking was named Hector and he was tall with a curly fade. He rode Othello's bike one too many times without giving it back to him, according to Sapphire. He didn't like this.

Othello knew these boys, but they didn't seem to show him much respect.

"Give it back, Hector, quit bugging," Othello said as Hector ignored him.

"One more run, lil dude," Hector said as he grinned at his goons who all wore the same thing as him: red Lettermen jackets and baggy jeans.

Was this a gang, thought Sapphire.

"He said give it back," he yelled.

Hector stopped.

"What, foo?" he said.

"I said...he said to give it back to him. It's his."

"No. What are you gone do about it?"

The wind stroked at Sapphire's hair. He stood up and said, "give it to him, now."

Hector pushed Othello's bike on the floor and grimaced as Sapphire squinted.

"You wanna go a round?" Hector asked.

Bullies: they took their power by using abuse, and inflicted pain on the week. He despised a bully more than his cheating father, more than his mother's tears, more than the look Othello had on his face when his bike was thrown to the ground.

Sapphire, with fist balled up, approached Hector and snatched a hair, an oily one, out of his head.

"Oooh," said Hector and his boys laughed. "He plucked my hair. I'm so scared."

"Sapphire, don't," said Othello as Sapphire stormed back into the apartment. He was in search of a doll, a voodoo doll, he had created from Leonidas's instructions.

Othello ran after him as he marched to his room.

124

"I had it handled," said Othello as Sapphire tied Hector's hair around a white makeshift doll with pencils for its skeleton.

"I hate a bully," said Sapphire. "By the power of my ancestors," Sapphire said as he clasped his hands together, just like Leonidas would.

Then, he took the doll and marched outside while Hector and his boys stood over Othello's bike talking.

He bent down as if he had been knocked backward. Sapphire gripped his doll with a grin as Hector Swayed from left to right as if being pulled by invisible strings.

"What are you doing?" One of his goons asked as he kept hopping around like an antique marionette performing for children.

Sapphire's eyes were full of Jubilation, almost a greediness in them for more fun. He was angry again, he hadn't felt that in a while.

Othello was the weaker one in this case, and that bothered him. He was without father, barely with mother and the gift his mother had provided had been thrown to the ground. Sapphire couldn't stand there while it happened. He had seen too many of them get off scott-free. Not today.

"I'm not doing nothing," Hector said, "that's him. He's a freak like everybody else in that building."

Sapphire hated name calling, he stuck his finger in the head of the doll and watched Hector cry out in pain.

A freak, Hector thought the magicians were freaks. How many people on the outskirts of Boon Hood knew about the uncanny practices that went on in the apartment Leonidas owned? Had Hector seen

Othello perform magic before? No one else from the other three apartment buildings called the magicians freaks but Hector seemed intolerable of it.

"Make it stop," said Hector as he began to slide in a 360 while making the most frantic face he could. "Come on man, please!"

Othello snickered, "Let him go, Sapphire. Enough, man."

"Aight," said Sapphire, snatching the hair from out of the tie on the doll, but not before making Hector slap one of his goons. "Get out of here, all of y'all!"

"Come on, man," said one of Hector's goons, "before he dishes out some more of that voodoo stuff on us."

All four of them ran like cowards, and Sapphire and Othello laughed and celebrated their victory.

"Ride your bike, man," said Sapphire, "I'm going in to get me some more cake."

"Cool," said Othello as he slapped hands with Sapphire. "Thanks again man, you always got my back."

"Yeah, man, just don't play around with those dudes no more. They not your real friends."

After receiving Sapphires advice, Othello rode his bike around and around. But after being bored, he rolled up the street to see Hector and his goons.

13 CLASH

Later that day, after more cake, Sapphire sat out on the front steps with Neptune and Napoleon. He had been eyeing a car in the center of the street that looked as if a man was loading drugs in its trunk.

This was a normal thing in Boon Hood, drug trafficking, Sapphire had noticed many times since being here.

Machiavelli's gang dealt heavy, and so did Crystal and his boys. The street that was between the four apartments was always full of people selling goods, drugs or even themselves. No one looked nervous about it either; Sapphire wondered why police never came to visit this neighborhood for inspections.

"Cops never come through here?" Sapphire asked as he looked over at Cirrus who had lit a cigarette.

"Nope," he said while inhaling, "too scared."

"Leonidas won't let any cop's come through here," said Neptune as she looked over to see that Crystal and Topaz had erected a basketball goal in the middle of the street.

"Why not, what did he do to them, pay them off?" asked Sapphire.

"Some of them, yeah," said Cirrus. "The others, who were trying to be a hero, were taught a lesson."

"Taught a lesson?" Sapphire squinted. "What do

127

you mean?"

"Leonidas protects us all, which is why he gets mad respect," said Cirrus. "He keeps us all out of the slammer and makes sure we all get to make our money. The way he sees it, the Man just wants to stop our hustle, but at the same time keep us from ever making it to the top. He ain't having it! You can come here and trade, sell and burrow without worrying about the Po' Po' –"

"But how does he do it?" asked Sapphire. "How does he teach them a lesson?"

"He's skilled in his voodoo," said Neptune, her hands rubbing together, "and can do very scary things with it. He can conjure these monsters called Eru's –"

"They're the worst," said Cirrus. "They have dark – black bodies and red slits for eyes. They can make you live out your scariest fears in your mind, over and over again."

"Leonidas had a list of cops that wouldn't give him a break, so his Eru's paid them all a visit. He talked to them all, the ones who couldn't be bribed and told them that he'd continue to invade their heads with mind numbing nightmares. They got the message, because clearly, they didn't come back to see us."

"Whoa," Sapphire whispered. "He really doesn't play games, huh?"

"Nope," said Cirrus as a limping Othello walked up to them with a black eye and a bloody nose."

"What happened to you?" Sapphire asked.

"It was them dudes, they took my bike and beat me up when I tried to get it back," said Othello.

"Sapphire, wait," said Neptune as she noticed that

Sapphire had sprung up.

"Take me to where they are," said Sapphire as he walked up to Othello.

"Let's get them busta's," said Cirrus as he hopped up and followed after the boys. "Neptune, stay here, and don't tell Leonidas where we going."

"Be safe, don't do anything stupid," said Neptune as she rubbed her sweater sleeves on her cheeks.

The three marched up the street, Othello wondering what Sapphire was going to do when he reached the gang's hang out. The clouds had gathered and the wind gusted through Sapphire's dreadlocks as he looked as if he could kill.

After walking three blocks, they approached a tall, white house that Othello had led them to. Inside, Hector sat back with his goons who all enjoyed puffs from various drugs, some giving off a strong stench.

The door swung open and startled him as Sapphire and his boys rushed in.

He jumped up, his girl, who was smoking with him, grinned as if she was about to be entertained.

"Where is his bike?" Sapphire said as he faced him, not showing any signs of fear. "Tell me now, or I'm gone –"

"Do what? I'm not afraid of y'all. I know what y'all are, freaks, you think your voodoo spiritual religion gone shake me? You wrong –"

"I don't have any voodoo tricks this time," said Sapphire as Hector dropped to the floor. "But if you test me again I'll show you my true power."

Hector clawed at his throat, looking as if he was choking on a golf ball. He had stirred up Sapphire who still hadn't mastered full control over his massive amount of power.

Cirrus popped his knuckles as Othello turned behind to see that they were becoming engulfed by Hector's goons.

"Um, Sapphire," said Cirrus, as his back touched Sapphire's, "we're kinda' surrounded."

"That's alright," said Sapphire as he swallowed deep, his stomach doing a somersault. "I ain't scared."

"Get them foo's," said Hector. "Take 'em all out!"

Sapphire turned his hand up at one guy and he flew upwards into the wall. Othello was shoved by another guy, but he was quickly intercepted by Cirrus's fist.

A tall, slim man punched Sapphire in his chest and regretted it when he was flown into a wall by Sapphire's telekinetic powers.

"We're outnumbered, man!" said Othello as he was tackled by two young boys.

"Massi Massi," said Cirrus, and suddenly five clones of himself appeared to join the fight, helping Othello become free from his bind.

One of the guys were Knocked unconscious by Cirrus's clone but another goon hit it so hard that it exploded into magical dust.

Now there was six versus the gang, and Hector had called for more to come in from the back porch.

Sapphire was reappearing everywhere, casting his spells from left to right. One man rushed at him with brute force.

"Bleximo!" Sapphire yelled and the man, along with two other guys behind him, were entangled in a glowing purple rope that had appeared from the tip of Sapphire's finger.

He turned to see that Cirrus's clones, which were helping him fight, were vanishing one by one after being hit too hard.

Hector came up towards Sapphire with a blade but he didn't look so tough after Sapphire cast his spell, "Glossus," and his tongue wrapped around his face three times.

That was a tricky jinx to learn for Sapphire, because he had to practice it on himself before getting it right. That wasn't very fun at all.

He had learned all these defense spells, due to the fact that New York streets were sometimes not very friendly.

He turned to Hector's lady who wanted a piece of the action for herself. Sapphire, not wanting to harm a female, cast a safe spell on her to avoid her. "Perista," he said as a flutter of doves appeared and carried her outside to land on the grass in the backyard.

Othello was thrown on the ground by a guy in a red windbreaker, Sapphire cast a spell with a loud roar, "Zalizmeno," while twirling his finger, he laughed as the guy spun around on his heel until he was completely dizzy.

But this wasn't enough; Cirrus was still taking on two guys who were younger than him but faster at their jabs and throws.

Sapphire ran to the kitchen and opened a utility closet. "Perfect," he said as he remembered the same spell that he had used to clean around the house back home. He raised his hands and said, "Zolum Fytro Antiko!"

A broom, a mop, and a vacuum flew from the closet and headed for the two men. Othello chuckled as he watched the two men become beat to a pulp by cleaning tools. The broom spanked, the mopped whacked and the vacuum came for the shins.

As three other men came downstairs looking for a fight, Sapphire wondered just how many men were jam-packed in this house. But, before Sapphire could conjure up another spell, a bright light, or more like a force field of green energy bombarded the house sending everyone flying backward, including the magicians.

From the door entered in Leonidas with his war staff in hand. He looked very serious, as Calypso and Neptune stood behind him.

"Sapphire, Cirrus, and Othello laid out on the floor with the goons while Leonidas walked in closer towards the center of the house.

"Boys, in the car, now!" he said as he thumped his staff on the carpet, this action causing Sapphire and the others to run out of the house immediately.

Leonidas didn't look like he was up for fun and games at this point, and neither did Calypso who seemed more worried than aggravated like Leonidas.

"Disobedience – your disobedience is out of control. That is why I treat you like I do," said Leonidas as Othello and Sapphire stood in the presence of Leonidas on the third floor while he stood in front of his throne. "Sapphire wouldn't have had to come and fight for you for the second time if you would have just stayed away from Hector's house like I told you, time after time. They don't love you like we do, they don't care like we do – they're not your friends, Othello. They kill their own kind if they have to, they're dirty. The black lung gang is vicious, and once again I had to pay to keep them quiet about what they saw!"

"I want to apologize about that part," said Sapphire, he looked up at Leonidas and then noticed Calypso who was standing behind the throne. "I was first to use magic against Hector, I'm sorry."

"That's alright, Sapphire, you were just standing up for Othello, like any of us would have done." Leonidas gestured to Cirrus who stood behind, along with Neptune and Napoleon who had just come from work. "But you wouldn't have to use your magic if he would have just told me that those boys were back down here – they're not supposed to be here after their Uncles did a drive-by down here last month and took out one of our old leaders. You play with fire! You always play with fire, Othello, and you wonder why I'm so overprotective over you, I'm afraid you're going to get yourself in so much trouble to where we can't get you out."

Othello looked down. Calypso shed a tear. Sapphire concluded that she did not like when things got heated in the apartment, especially not on a day like today.

"Sapphire told you to stay away from them, he also told you not to try to transform anything living – aye dios mio, we could have all been eaten alive by that monster because you don't listen. I know I'm not your father, but I'm a darn good big brother, who took you in and raised you when your mother didn't want you – I deserve some kind of respect, I deserve for you to listen to something that I tell you!"

Leonidas paused as a tear fell from Othello's face this time.

Then, while taking his seat on his throne, he said, "because it's your birthday, I won't put you on chore duty…but just chill out in your room until our lessons tonight. I need a break from you right now, Othello."

Sapphire watched as Othello walked off and took the steps down to the second floor.

"Was I too harsh, sister?" Leonidas asked as Calypso put her hand on his shoulder.

"No, no," said Calypso, "you're okay, he needed that. And I don't want you apologizing to him later on, he really needed to hear that, brother."

"I know. But that's my baby. That's my baby, Calypso, I just…." Leonidas looked as if his eyes were beginning to water. "Sapphire, go talk to him, please, try to cheer 'em back up if you can."

"Okay," said Sapphire as he turned on his heels to head towards the steps down to the second floor.

This apartment building and its inhabitants were so interesting to Sapphire. The level of love and family, and compassion, and strength that resided in these halls was amazing. He respected the relationship between Leonidas and his people, that he loved.

A black man, a young black man, had taken over as king over a neighborhood, and Sapphire could tell that he was trying his best to be the best King he could be, the best family man he could be, and the best big brother he could be.

After Sapphire talked to him with reasoning and jokes, he was able to get him going again. The two laughed about the fight from earlier, both of them admitting that they had never been in something like that before.

It was a rush for the both of them, and maybe more fun than endangering.

14 CLAIRVOYANCE

Sapphire taught after lunch and everyone attended, except Cirrus, who was down in his room arguing with his brother over the phone. Othello mentioned in their lesson that he had been trying to find his father's number but his brother wouldn't give it to him, due to his unforgiving ways.

Today's lesson was focused on animating inanimate objects. Sapphire had been asked to teach the spell after Othello bragged about how cool it looked when they fought the Black Lung gang.

When the lessons were done, Sapphire and Othello watched Home Alone in Neptune's room on her VHS.

Inside her room were pictures of her favorite actresses. She had a tall dresser with love letters from old lovers, dried roses, perfume bottles and miscellaneous makeup cases placed on its surface.

The boys sat on her bed as she painted her toes. Her Christmas lights were hung everywhere and buzzed bright pink, instead of their usual blue at night. She had changed their color for a more daytime setting.

Othello had begged to watch the movie in her room because her television was the biggest. They laughed so hard while watching it that Leonidas came down to see what all the outbursts were for.

When he walked in, he had Nekita around his neck.

"Please don't come in here with that thing," said Neptune as she backed away.

"She's alright," said Leonidas as he kissed his snake in the mouth. "She don't like other females, mami, you don't have to worry."

"I'm out of here," said Neptune as she got up from her bed. "I'm about to go have my reading done."

"A reading?" said Sapphire.

"Yeah, Calypso's going to do it," said Neptune, grabbing a fifty dollar bill from her wallet.

"She never does them because it takes a lot of her energy, but, if you beg she'll give in," said Leonidas.

"Can we come watch?" Sapphire asked. "I've never been to a reading."

"Yeah, come on," said Neptune as she threw on a red button down to cover her undershirt.

"Where y'all going?" asked Napoleon as he came downstairs in a white T and jeans.

"Calypso's having a reading," said Othello as everyone walked down the hall.

"Cool, I'm coming," Napoleon said.

Everyone walked into Calypso's room and marveled at all the African art she had along her walls. Her bed had a purple veil over it with more than enough silk pillows of all sizes. She sat at a round table with her hair in a white wrap. She wore bright red lipstick with dark eyeliner. Her nails were the same red as her dress that flowed to the floor.

"Thanks for doing this for me," Neptune said as she handed Calypso her money.

"Any time," said Calypso, rolling her eyes, "you know how much I love doing this. Sit down, please. Everybody else just stay out of the way. Don't talk either."

Neptune sat, facing Calypso, and between them was a crystal ball.

Sapphire imagined that Calypso had been asked to do this many times, judging by her facial expressions.

"Okay," said Calypso as she waved her hand by a candle, causing it to burn bright.

She looked into her crystal ball as it turned many different colors. She looked up at Neptune. "You want the whole shebang – past, present, future –?"

"Yes," said Neptune, smiling. "Please."

"Okay," said Calypso, breathing hard. "Your past foretells of…of lost, and…rebellion, hopelessness, homelessness – you were rejected by your Christian parents for a lover of yours that they didn't approve of, his views very unorthodox, but it wasn't real love, only a game."

Neptune placed her hand over her shoulder. "Mmmhmm."

Calypso continued on as her crystal ball turned from green to blue to yellow. Sapphire wondered what these colors meant. "Your present tells me that you've found family, after being exiled by your own, and you're grateful – not wanting to ever leave their affection. You want love, but not just from family but from a man, a man of a different shade than yours, his background different from yours – but his future intertwined with yours."

Calypso shuttered, was reading this Crystal Ball affecting her health, Sapphire thought. She caressed it some more, her eyes squinting as if she was trying to look through a keyhole.

She continued on and said, "he attracts you, feeds your soul with his words and kind smile but you don't think he notices you when you walk by or try to speak. Your future has love involved – and I can't see from who – but you will take part in both love, and despair. Celebration and destruction, gathering and lost –"

Calypso stopped. "I hate doing this."

"No, its fine, I know it isn't always going to be good, keep going," said Neptune. "I don't care what happens…especially not since I know I'll have love – that's all I want. Come on."

"I can't," said Calypso as she raised her hands and caused a towel to fly in her grips. She was sweating badly. "I hate seeing the negative, that's why I stopped looking in this thing. I can't control what I see in it like Madam Celeste can, or like my mother could. It just doesn't like me."

"You're doing fine," said Leonidas as she stroked Nekita. "You've got this.

Calypso shook her head in disagreement.

"Well, if you're done reading…can you at least help me contact my grandmother who passed last year –?"

"Now you know I can't do that," said Calypso as she looked at Neptune. "Once a spirit crosses over, there's nothing I can do, they're off limits to me – because they're Gods property now. All those séances you see on TV are fake."

139

"That isn't what you used to tell people back in the day," said Leonidas as he jabbed at Napoleon who apparently knew what he was talking about. "Sapphire," he said as he chuckled, "Calypso used to make bread off of folks – she'd bring them in here and have séances, acting all stupid, rolling her eyes and shaking. I see your mother, she says hello from beyond the grave."

Everyone burst in tears as Calypso threw her towel at Leonidas.

"Shut up," said Calypso. "I had to make my money, dude."

No one laughed anymore as Cirrus walked in with his eyes glossy, wearing his usual leather jacket and tight jeans. He approached Neptune and said, "move."

"What?" said Neptune.

"Can you move please?!" Cirrus said, making Neptune jerk.

"Okay, gosh, what's wrong with you?" she asked as she got up from her seat and let him take her place.

He eyed Calypso as if she had stolen his cigarettes.

"Cirrus, what's wrong?" Leonidas asked. "You wanna go talk about it, man?"

Cirrus ignored Leonidas. "I need to know about my father, Calypso –"

"Now you know I don't do nothing for free," said Calypso.

"My father was found in Dallas, under a bridge, high on pills and cocaine," said Cirrus, his eyes now dripping with tears. "My mom said they rushed him to the hospital but it ain't lookin' good. Is he or is he not going to die?"

Calypso gathered herself and looked over at Leonidas. She placed her hands on the crystal ball and focused.

The crystal ball was feeding her information – but maybe too forcefully because she made a sour expression. "Your father...flesh of your flesh...born of a railroad worker and a housemaid."

Calypso stopped. Leonidas moved closer towards her as she looked as if her energy was leaving her. "He abandoned his woman for drugs and traded his children for the thrill of alcohol and gambling.

His children waited for their father but he never came back. They searched but he didn't want to be found. He slumped over benches, passed out in the streets, filled his belly with alcohol disease and now he –"

The candle lost its light, Calypso grabbed ahold of her mouth and Leonidas looked to see what Cirrus would do.

"And now," said Calypso as she looked directly into Cirrus' eyes, "and now he sleeps. I'm so sorry, Cirrus."

"What?" said Cirrus as he looked at Calypso.

"I'm so sorry, so sorry, Cirrus," Calypso said as tears fell from her eyes.

Cirrus squinted his eyes. "You saying he's dead – you saying he didn't make it?!" Cirrus slapped Calypso's crystal ball off its harness. "Man, forget this crap, you don't know what you're talking about, man – you don't know!"

Leonidas let Nekita slither on the ground, and she exited out the door as he jumped to grab a hold of Cirrus who had now collapsed over Calypso's table in a crying fit.

"Its okay, its okay," said Leonidas as he held onto Cirrus, his eyes leaking as well.

"That's my pops man, that's my pops man," Cirrus said as he cried out in muffled rants. "Y'all don't understand."

"We understand," said Leonidas as he gripped Cirrus' body, his head beside his. Everyone else quickly gathered around in a group hug, including Calypso who couldn't stop crying herself.

He was engulfed with love and could not resist it. Everyone cared and he knew it, but the pain wouldn't let him give in, he shot up with his face red as an apple. "Get off me, man, get off me!"

"Cirrus," said Neptune.

"I'm so sorry," said Calypso as she watched Cirrus stumble across the hall to his room. He fell to the floor and cried his eyes out.

Leonidas waved his hand towards Cirrus' door, "he wants to be alone," he said as the door closed itself.

Everyone scattered, except for Sapphire and Calypso, who stood on both sides of Leonidas as he looked at Cirrus' door.

Leonidas wrapped his arms around Sapphire and Calypso, as he released a tear from his eye. "His father never took care of him…but he still needs him…and now he's gone."

Crying fits echoed throughout the hall for a little while, after everyone had rested in their rooms. An hour later, Leonidas gathered everyone and knocked on Cirrus' door.

"What?" said Cirrus.

"Can we come in…please?" said Leonidas.

A few seconds passed, and afterward, the door opened itself to reveal Cirrus leaning against his bed with dark circles under his eyes.

Leonidas walked in as everyone else stayed behind. "We made something for you. We know it ain't much but Calypso knows how much you like chocolate cake so we baked you one – if you would like to come downstairs with us – I'm sorry if I'm intruding, man –"

"Nope," said Cirrus. "You aight, B. It don't matter…I'm good."

"I know you hurting," said Calypso, "but you don't have to go through it alone."

"Come on," said Leonidas as he helped Cirrus up, "get up, man, I can't leave my brother hanging like this, man. It's gone be alright, we love you."

"I love y'all…." Cirrus said.

"Before we go downstairs," Leonidas said, "we wanted to show you something."

Upon the third floor, with everyone together, Leonidas walked to a middle room in the hall that had African markings on the door in a foreign language. The door opened itself and inside was a shelled out apartment with concrete for a floor instead of carpet. No drywall was up, just slabs of more concrete and small memorials that were propped up underneath the windows. One was labeled Osiris Agbara and it

143

was covered in small candles, flowers, and African trinkets. Next to it was a memorial for Leonidas's mother and across was for more deceased relatives of Leonidas's family.

Cirrus was led to a memorial for his own father. Everyone had left handmade cards and placed them by roses that Calypso had put down. Leonidas took chalk from his pocket and handed it to Cirrus. "I come here to remember my ancestors. This is my secret place...where I can talk to them and tell them all of my problems. This is now opened to you...write your father's name on the wall.

Cirrus wrote his father's name: Harold Black, and tried to fight back tears while doing so.

Sapphire had left a small poem for Cirrus who bent down to read it. Everyone stood over him as he used his little strength left to light a candle in front of him.

"It's okay to cry," said Leonidas as he placed his hand on Cirrus' shoulder.

Sapphire bent down with Cirrus and so did Othello.

"You wanna say anything to 'em?" said Leonidas as he looked down at Cirrus. "I talk to my father all the time. Don't feel ashamed."

"Dad...I'ma miss you," said Cirrus. "I know I didn't have a relationship with you, but I really wanted one...but you wouldn't let me...you wouldn't give me a chance...man."

Leonidas rubbed Cirrus' back as he continued to cry out.

Napoleon walked out, being too proud to show his tears. Neptune took off a shawl from her back and placed it around Cirrus. "You're gonna get through, tough guy.

Fatherhood was an essential part of anyone's life, according to Sapphire.

He had had his father but had regretted the spiteful words he used against him. What if his father had died today like Cirrus' had? What if he had never gotten a chance to say goodbye, would he have been just as down as Cirrus was? Fathers were the backbone, in Sapphire's family. Although they were not perfect, they stepped in and did their part, just like the mothers did.

Leonidas felt Cirrus' pain, and this was evident because Sapphire could see the familiarity in Leonidas's eyes as if he wanted to cry in his place. He had his father, just like Sapphire did, a strong man, a king. He had lost his as well.

"Fathers are the reason we men are how we are," said Leonidas as he caressed Cirrus' back. "They help make us who we are if they're in our life or not. They help mold us. I'm so sorry for your...I'm so sorry, Cirrus."

After the memorial, everyone ate Calypso's cake in the kitchen. No one cried but laughed as Cirrus told stories of his father. Everyone had seemed to cheer him up.

"He would, he would beat the devil out of us kids when he WAS around," Cirrus said as he stuffed his face with cake. "But we stayed in these duplexes, in Georgia, so, the boys across us cut a hole in the wall — they knew when we would get beat by our pops that

145

we would run under our iron bed, we had an iron bed, and we'd run under it. Pops would run in after us and swing at us while we were under the bed."

Everyone laughed as Cirrus could barely swallow while he told his story. "So the boys cut a hole in the wall across from us so when we'd get whipped we'd run under our bed and crawl through the hole. Now pops would get to swinging that belt, but we'd start fake crying like we was getting hit – but we was right across the hall in another apartment!"

Everyone irrupted in laughter and Cirrus continued his jokes about his father that he could remember.

Fatherhood: a journey Sapphire had learned so much about from so many different people. He didn't know if he wanted children but knew that when he did he'd have to learn from every bad father's mistakes. He missed his dad. Not enough to call but enough to remember the times he spent with him, like learning to shoot a gun, tie his shoes and spell his name.

Father's everywhere had an impact on their children, and Sapphire didn't think the world knew just how many thugs, pimps, gangsters and hooligans would have lived better if they had a Papa to call their own.

This chapter is specially dedicated to my grandmother, Connie B. Graham, who lost her father. You'll soon see him again in heaven.

15 GATHERING

The morning of the celebration went very well, especially since Calypso cooked steak and eggs for breakfast, Leonidas' favorite.

Everyone clicked and clanged, buttered toast, smacked and grinned as plates of scrambled eggs kept flying in after Calypso, who brought in a pitcher of Orange juice.

Yesterday was cold cereal day, and Sapphire didn't really like cereal all that much so today's bountiful feast of a breakfast made him very happy.

"Hey, everyone, what's the one thing that everybody at this table has in common?" asked Neptune as she looked around at everyone.

"We're all magicians, duh," said Cirrus as Othello snickered.

Neptune shot a deadly look at Cirrus. "Can you guys think of anything else?"

"We don't have any children," said Calypso.

"Excellent," said Neptune, "we don't have any children. None of us."

"Well, do you want kids?" Napoleon asked.

"Of course, said" Neptune. "I want a lot of children."

"I don't," said Cirrus. "I'll be an Uncle but that's it, fam."

"Yeah, same for me," said Othello, "I don't want kids."

"You too young to even be talking about kids," said Leonidas.

"Well, what about you?" asked Calypso as she peeked over at Leonidas.

"What about me?"

"Do you want kids?"

"I need to find a woman first before the baby comes – that's kinda how it works."

"Why don't you have a lady yet?" asked Neptune.

"I've been through this with Calypso before," said Leonidas. "The last time I had a girl it ended horribly. This chic from The Bronx ruined my life."

"But that was last year, Leonidas," said Calypso. "You've had all of 96 to find a Queen for your kingdom."

"Ion' know," said Leonidas, "I guess girls just don't find me attractive."

"Lies," said Calypso as everyone snickered. "You're very handsome, boy."

Leonidas smiled, "yeah, but I'm a tall string bean and I don't have big muscles and I don't have a big butt, girls love guys with a nice butt –"

Everyone irrupted in laughter.

"What's so funny?" said Neptune. "I know I do. I love a guy with a nice butt –"

"Can we stop talking about dudes butts, please," said Cirrus.

"Really, women are just as into the backside as men are," said Calypso. "A guy with a lil something, something."

"And a beard," said Neptune. "He's gotta' have a beard and height, which Leonidas has, and I need him to have muscles though, girl."

"Mmmhmm," said Calypso as she sipped her orange juice.

"See, wait a minute," said Leonidas, "how is it that a woman can mention all the things a guy has to have, in the way she likes it, but if a man does the same thing he's a pig?"

"Right, right," said Cirrus.

"Yeah," said Sapphire, "It's like, I'm wrong for saying I need my girl to have hair, long hair, and of course I'm a dog for that – but, but if a woman says her guy has to have a beard she's just listing her preferences."

"Preach," said Leonidas.

"It's almost like we're wrong for catcalling, but if you think about it, girls do the same thing," said Sapphire. "I used to work at a gym, I know, when they see a guy walk by they can 'ooh and awww' and yell out what they'd do to him –"

"But if we do it, we're pigs," said Leonidas.

"Well, women can have preferences," said Calypso.

"Yes, but, why can't men?" asked Leonidas.

Neptune giggled. "Because...men are dogs."

"And what are women, cats?" Sapphire said. "Either way, we're both animals."

The debate carried on further until the food stopped coming. No one got their points across fully, due to objections and loud laughter. Table talk was always this good when everyone didn't have to rush off and go anywhere. They argued like any other family but it was never negative. Leonidas had been successful at creating an environment where everyone could be heard and have a chance to share how they felt

As the sun began to set, everyone got dressed and prepared for a wonderful night. Leonidas seemed to be really excited about the gathering and so was Othello who had talked about all the food that Machiavelli's mother was going to prepare for tonight. Neptune did Calypso's make up in her room and she returned the favor by letting her borrow her distressed fishnets to wear.

Napoleon was constantly coming out of his room in just his towel while displaying shirts that he wanted approval for. Cirrus blasted his 2Pac while getting ready and Sapphire re-twisted his dreadlocks in his bathroom as Othello harassed him with questions on his hair.

"So, Leonidas does this big, dramatic entrance," said Othello, behind Sapphire, in his restroom, "where everybody bows as he comes in and he gives a speech and all – but after that, we get to feast and dance, dance, dance!"

"Sounds cool to me," said Sapphire as he took out metal clips that were clasping his roots. "How's the speech, is it long?"

"No, he's not really a talker. He sits at the head of

the table and just says some encouraging type stuff."

Everyone had their door open and Sapphire could hear Neptune screaming at Napoleon for his constant need to know what shirt looked good on him as Calypso threatened to hex Cirrus if he didn't turn his music down.

"You're just gonna wear the same leather jacket over it like you always do, bum!" said Neptune.

"Hey, cool your jets," said Leonidas as he came downstairs from his room. He knocked on Sapphire's door and leaned his head in. "Sapphire, may I speak to you…upstairs, in my room?"

Sapphire looked over at Othello as he pulled the last silver clip from his dreadlocks. "Sure, no problem."

"Thank you," said Leonidas as Sapphire walked out of his room with Othello following behind. "I wish to speak to Sapphire alone, my young Prince," said Leonidas as he placed his hand on Othello's shoulder with a wide grin on his face.

"Okay," said Othello.

"We won't be long," said Leonidas as Sapphire walked upstairs with him to his room on the third floor. The voodoo king had an identical apartment to Sapphire's but the inhabitants were very different. Inside were wooden, beaded, feather-adorned mask all around the walls that were painted a shade of green on some walls and then salmon on the others. A dresser with many fragrances and a round mirror on it sat over to the left with a statue of a mighty leopard displayed on its wooden surface by some rosary beads.

The carpet was cheetah, the ceiling fan was

151

decorated with dream catchers and candles were on a glass table with a skull and a deck of what appeared to be fortune telling cards. Leonidas' bed had purple curtains around it, and a picture to the left of his mother and father in their older years hung by the wall beside it.

More pictures of loved ones, to the right, were hung on a salmon colored wall above a short rack of fancy dress shoes; some with spikes, others with fur.

"I can't decide between the fur…and the spiked shoes," said Leonidas.

He had on a white T and skinny, black leather pants, but nothing was on his feet. "I always wear my mother's fur and my father's necklace of elephant tusk…but my shoe preference always changes up on me."

"Well, maybe you should just go barefoot this time," chuckled Sapphire as Leonidas cracked a smile.

"Good idea, brotha', but I have to walk across the street, and if you haven't noticed its cold outside."

"Well, I like the spiked ones," said Sapphire. "Really."

"Okay, cool, I'll go with 'em. Since you're my consultant I'm gonna take your advice."

"Consultant?"

"Yes," said Leonidas, his bushy eyebrow raised. "I brought you up here to offer you the royal position as my armor bearer, my consultant…and not only that but my bodyguard."

"Bodyguard?" said Sapphire.

"Mmmhmm," said Leonidas, as he walked over to his mirror to pick out his afro. "In this last week, you have shown great power, kind-heartedness, love, and great wisdom. You're everything a king could want in a bodyguard. I'd be honored to put my life in your hands, I don't care if you're just twenty. You're a mature man...a handsome, strong, black magician with great talent."

"But...you didn't already have a bodyguard before I came?"

"Well, no. Sapphire, I never thought I'd live to see two superior spell casters in my life and...and when I discovered you were one I took it as a sign that a worthy armor bearer was finally here. I mean, none of them downstairs are as powerful as you, although they're all very special to me – they don't have what you've got."

"But, why do I have what I've got?" Sapphire asked. "Why was I chosen to have this power?"

"Listen," said Leonidas, his hands on Sapphire's shoulders, "my father said that a superior spell caster has great power that exists in the bloodline of his or her family. It courses through their entire lineage but only chooses to stay in the body that can hold it... that can possess it. Someone from your bloodline was a superior and now you have received their power. Some call it the theory of everlasting love...the force that moves through a family; very strong magic, Sapphire."

"Well, I can't turn down your offer," said Sapphire. "You have done so much for me...."

"You know, my father wouldn't let anyone be his bodyguard...he said in order for him to be properly guarded he would only put his life in the hands of another superior. I guess I took after him."

"But I just –"

"Look, I would never put a lot on you," said Leonidas. "I don't want you thinking I'm sending you on some dangerous mission, but I just need someone to have my back, that's all. And I trust you and love you like a brother. You've given so much to Osiris in just the week you've been here. And I hope to grow with you, like I've grown with everyone else."

"I can't say no, Leonidas," Sapphire said, his hands gripping Leonidas's shoe rack. "Of course."

"Great," said Leonidas, he wrapped his arms around Sapphire, his scent of strong spices over him. "Take my hand, brother." Sapphire reached out and joined hands with Leonidas. "I swear to be your king, a noble king, a loving king. Do you swear to be my loyal consultant, the guardian of my throne?"

"I swear," said Sapphire, his stomach feeling as if it was overbearingly filled with a hot liquid. Leonidas had love in his heart, Sapphire could feel it. He didn't need to be a psychic like Calypso to know that all Leonidas wanted to do was love and be loved. He had passion; his eye's revealed that to Sapphire.

This felt good, the unity between brothers, the bond of friendship; the kindred spirits.

"This is great, great," said Leonidas with a shy smile. He had grown man features but a child-like smile that could light up a room. He turned to his mirror and picked at his afro more. "I have to give a speech on the third floor tonight; I would be honored to have you at the congregation table beside me...with all the other leaders of the apartments. Oh, and please wear that black hat I got you, it just makes you look even more like the brilliant magician you are."

"Sure," said Sapphire.

"Cool. So, in about another hour, we're gonna head out. I have to be escorted out with my, well, I don't have a woman yet so I'm walking out with Calypso –"

"Why don't you have a woman, again? If you don't mind?"

"Well, I used to," Leonidas said. "Two years ago... she was sweet. Her name was Autumn. I liked her a lot, I did, man. But, we just didn't want the same things in life."

"Really?" Sapphire looked at Leonidas as he applied lotion to his face.

"She wanted to leave Boon Hood and start a new life on the west coast, she was a cousin of Machiavelli's, and was tired of being down here. I chose to stay when she moved; I could never leave my father's kingdom...my people...my home."

"If you ever found another girl what would you want her to be like...look like?"

"Hmmm," Leonidas tapped at his chin, "I like chocolate sista's; daaark chocolate...beautiful. And, hopefully, she can...sing. I think it is so attractive when a girl can sing –"

"SHE'S HERE!" yelled Calypso from downstairs.

Suddenly, Leonidas leaped from his room, down the steps, Sapphire following behind. In a puff of black smoke, a woman stood with blond hair tied in three buns: two on both sides of her head and one at the top. She looked mid-forties and had on a black ankle length dress with a bundle of Christmas lights around her neck as an accessory, Sapphire wondering how they were lighted. She had high heeled platform boots that were a bright pink and her lips were dark

155

black.

Calypso, Othello, and Neptune stood around her as if she was a warm fire on a cold day as she stood with a bright smile on her face. As Leonidas approached her she curtsied with a slight tilt.

"Magenta," said Leonidas as he hugged the woman that Sapphire had never seen before. "Calypso told me you'd be here!"

"Yeah, well, the psychic has to always ruin the surprises, huh?" Magenta said her voice a cartoonish squeak that almost made Sapphire laugh as he stood behind Leonidas.

"Hey, guy's, I'm just going with the leather – oh, dude, it's Magenta!" said Napoleona he entered in.

"Duh," said Neptune.

"Magenta's here?" asked Cirrus, as he stepped out of his room.

"Magenta, I want you to meet Sapphire," said Leonidas as he placed a hand on Sapphire's shoulder, "my consultant and my bodyguard. And Sapphire, this is Magenta, one of the original women who moved into Osiris under the care of my parents – before I could even walk."

"Pleasure to meet cha'," said Magenta, shaking Sapphire's hand very firmly.

"Nice to meet you," said Sapphire.

"He's a poet," said Leonidas.

"Ah, really?" said Magenta.

"And, the best part, he's a superior spell caster," said Leonidas.

Magenta gasped. "No way, shut up! Like, you mean like your father?"

"Yup," said Calypso, smiling at Sapphire. He

noticed that her hair was covered in a head wrap of fancy, golden material to match the golden dashiki dress she wore with bronze embroidered flowers. "He can do wonders, Magenta, he's out of this world."

Sapphire didn't know how to handle all of these compliments.

"Sapphire, Magenta always visits us on the day of the Brethren Gathering to show her love – and to show us new magic that she's learned from all the places she visits," said Leonidas. "Besides you, her and my father was the only ones to master teleportation."

"Wow," said Sapphire, he loved being around his fellow spell casters, the more, the merrier he was.

"Oh, man, I've been dying to show you all this one I've learned from my weekend in Louisiana," said Magenta. "Some magician at a floral shop sold it to me for cheap. Everybody, into Othello's room, it's been forever since I've been in my old room, gosh."

"Let's go!" said Leonidas, his smile broadening.

"Oh, Calypso, can you bring me a candle, from your room, doll?"

"Sure," said Calypso as she waved her hand and a long, blue candle flew from out of her room and into her hand. "Here you go."

"Thank you," said Magenta as she grasped the blue candle from Calypso's hand. Everyone crowded around in Othello's room and some sat on his bed as others stood behind Magenta, who faced Calypso as if she was about to ask her a serious question.

"Louisiana was beautiful," Magenta said. "I traveled from New Orleans, Shreveport and down to Minden, where I learned this nifty spell. I love your

157

beautiful, hazel eyes, Calypso, but have you ever wanted them BLUE?"

"No way," whispered Othello, his mouth wide open.

"You can change her eye color?" Neptune asked, biting her fingernail.

"Yes, my darling, watch and learn," said Magenta as she gripped the blue candle tightly, her eyes closing. She passed the candle to Calypso and told her to repeat the words, "Viso Eiello Candellebro."

"Viso Eiello Candellebro," said Calypso, her lips moving precisely so that she could properly pronounce the words. After reciting her incantation, all of the candles blue color seemed to be drawn out of it; its wax became a milky white as the candle's flame blew out and Calypso's eyes became a beautiful blue, as deep as the sea.

"Perfect," said Magenta as she turned Calypso towards Othello's tall mirror on his wall.

"You're amazing, Magenta," Leonidas said, his chin on his fist.

"Super dope," said Othello and Cirrus.

"Wow, I look so…different," said Calypso as everyone giggled out of excitement. "This is so cool. How…how long does it last, Magenta?"

"Twenty four hours," said Magenta with a grin. "Then you're back to normal."

"Does it work on red candles?" Neptune asked, her eyes looking over at Magenta.

"Oh, well, yeah, but d'you really want red eyes, Neptune –"

"Why not!?"

"No matter what you try, you're not gonna get

Crystal to notice you tonight," said Napoleon as he smirked at Neptune.

"Shut up, jerk," said Neptune.

"You'll get his attention tonight, Neptune," said Calypso as she exited from Othello's room with Leonidas. "Trust me...I'm a psychic."

"Sweet, thanks Calypso" said Neptune. "Bite me, Napoleon."

Magenta had walked upstairs to discuss something with Leonidas, Othello and the other boys went downstairs with Neptune and Calypso as Sapphire finished getting dressed in his room. He slid into a black T, blue skinny jeans and some black, high top boots that Cirrus had given him. He placed his black fedora hat over his dreads, and as he walked out of his room, he heard Leonidas and Magenta coming back downstairs.

"Sapphire, Sapphire," said Magenta. "I just spoke with Leonidas about tonight's gathering, and I wanted to ask him if you'd perform one of your poems for us all – after Leonidas gives his speech?"

"Uh, what...yeah," said Sapphire as he saw the hope in Magenta's eyes. He didn't feel comfortable reading his poetry at such short notice, but he didn't think it was a very difficult thing to do. "I'll go get one of them."

"Excellent," said Leonidas as he stood behind Magenta with a wide smile. "And when you come downstairs, we're all gonna head out. Okay?"

"Cool," said Sapphire.

After retrieving a poem that he had written last night, before falling into a long, awaited sleep, Sapphire walked downstairs and could see that

159

everyone was ready. Cirrus in his usual black stood by Napoleon in his usual black as Neptune went for a more distressed look than usual. Othello wore a red sweater and jeans and stood behind Magenta who was behind Calypso and Leonidas, who had on his mother's fur and a necklace of elephant tusk adorning it.

"Sapphire, you stand right here, behind Leonidas," said Magenta as Sapphire assumed his place behind Leonidas, his hair smelling very fruity tonight. "As his armor bearer, you've got to be by his side."

"Of course," said Sapphire with a big swallow.

Earlier, he could see out of the upstairs window, by the steps that many people were walking into the apartment across the street. Was he ready to be around so many people, was he prepared to perform in front of them all?

"Everyone," said Leonidas, "let's go have a great time like its 1999!"

The door sprung open, this time by Leonidas's own magic. The voodoo king, with a proud look upon his face, walked out with Calypso beside him, her arm under his as if he was leading her to be married. With dignity, the magicians made their way towards Machiavelli's apartment. Many were outside waiting for them, smiles on their faces as they watched the magicians stretch across the street with Calypso and Leonidas leading them. A man with bright skin and a brown flat cap that matched his pea coat opened the door to the apartment.

"Hello, Pierre," said Leonidas, with a humble smile.

"That's Crystal and Topaz's dad," said Othello,

behind Sapphire's ear. "He's a killer sax player, you've got to hear dude play."

Sapphire could see past Leonidas's afro that many people were dancing in the hallway of the apartment to very loud music. Some jumping, some head bobbing.

"Evening, your majesty," Pierre said as he led the magicians in, and as he did, the crowd began to part and everyone either slid back into the rooms of the hall or kneeled as he said, "All hail the King of Boon Hood, his Royal Highness, Leonidas Osiris Agbara, of the Royal Agbara clan."

This was magnificent in Sapphire's eyes to see so many men and women who seemed juvenile (because of their clothing) because of their appearance, show so much reverence and bow so humbly. A few of the men that Sapphire had seen act barbaric in the streets or sell drugs on corners were kneeled down as if they were honored to give honor to the king of their neighborhood.

Leonidas had said earlier, during share, that the other three leader's parents were the ones that kept the royal traditions alive, as he himself felt odd about asking people to bow to him, but Pierre, who claimed to be the closest friend to Osiris, made sure the neighborhood kept their respects in order.

Walking through the hall of River was a little different than over at Osiris: the hallway was even wider, no table sat in the middle and the rooms were larger and packed with people dancing in them. Everyone made their way to the third floor of the apartment after seeing that the second floor was just as packed as the first. On the third floor was a long table with food spread all around it. At least two Turkey's, two hams, a slab of ribs, greens, cabbage, corn and many other edible goods were stacked around the table.

"I told you, Patience, Machiavelli's mom, makes the best stuff, man," said Othello as a woman with dark skin, an ear length bob, and an oversized tan sweater placed a plate of fried chicken on the table.

"Machiavelli," she said, "the king is here!"

Everyone slowly made their way around the table as Leonidas took his head seat and asked Sapphire to sit on his right side and Calypso to sit on his left, by Magenta. The rest of the gang stood behind Leonidas as Pierre sat down next, by a bright skinned woman with long braids sprouting all around the top of her head and black shades over her eyes.

"Is that Alexandrite?" Sapphire whispered as he looked behind himself towards Othello. "The one with the dark glasses?"

"Yup," said Othello, "and that's her man by her and personal bodyguard. He was the one that turned her. They're both as mean as a rattlesnake."

"I heard that," said Alexandrite, her fingers gripping each other. Beside her was a man, with dark shades and a tall build, a smirk creeping across his face as Othello whispered that he was sorry.

Sapphire wondered if Alexandrite's bodyguard was doing his job right after hearing that he had turned her into a vampire, which only happened after biting into one's neck.

"My brotha'!" said a man with long dreadlocks that were in a ponytail and darker than his brown skin complexion. He wore an army coat over a black sweater and had a purple charm bracelet around his wrist.

"Machiavelli," said Leonidas as he beckoned for a pitcher of orange juice to float over to him, "you know, mom really made a slammin' dinner, all this looks wonderful. Y'all show great hospitality."

"Awww, it's my pleasure," Patience said as she took her seat beside Sapphire while Machiavelli sat at the foot. Many men and women who seemed as if they were Machiavelli's supporters stood behind him as a man introduced as Aristotle (who was a very chubby, gray-haired man) sat next to Patience.

"Where's the wife?" Leonidas asked as he drank his orange juice from a glass goblet with green jewels around it.

"She's sick, your highness," Aristotle said as he looked around to see who all was at the table.

"Well, me and my consultant will be by your apartment tomorrow to heal her," Leonidas said.

"Thank you, King Leonidas," said Aristotle with a generous smile. "Thank you."

"Does all of our guests have food downstairs as well?" asked Leonidas. "I wanna make sure everybody eats."

"Sure," said Machiavelli, "me and mom served everyone earlier in the main kitchen downstairs. And they were all checked thoroughly by my men, before entering in, no new faces. My most trusted bodyguards are patrolling and they guard with their lives. Everyonee's checked for the witch hunter tattoo as well."

Witch hunter tattoo, Sapphire thought. He had never heard of such a thing. He had been informed by his mother that there was a group of hunters that killed witches and sorcerers in the 70's but everyone said they had all died off.

"Excellent, fantastic," said Leonidas as a tall, bright skinned, broad-shouldered man walked in, his green eyes looking around at everyone that had beat him to the table.

"Greetings, King," he said with a shy smile as he sat at the right side of Machiavelli, at the foot of the table.

It was Crystal and Topaz, walking in behind him.

"Hey, there he is," said Leonidas as a smile arose on his face. "Now, we can begin the feast since the mighty Crystal is here."

Machiavelli busted out in tears, even Alexandrite cracked a smile and Crystal and Pierre laughed: this made Sapphire feel as if Leonidas was being very sarcastic with his words. There was an inside joke here that he didn't know about.

"Everyone began to serve themselves as plates were traded, scooted and served around. Those that stood behind Leonidas and Machiavelli all received their plates and either stood and ate or sat on the steps downstairs.

Leonidas cleared his throat as everyone shifted their attention to him. The clanking and clattering of dinner wear ceased as he opened his mouth to say, "it gives me great pleasure to be here at our 28th Brethren Gathering. I can only hope for many more years...our 30th anniversary...our 50th."

"That's right," whispered Patience. The Brethren Gathering seemed just as important to her as it was to Leonidas.

"We want to honor our fallen brother," said Leonidas. "River, another brother gone but never forgotten. We lost him to a shootout with the Black Lung gang that came through two months ago – and I assure you that we'll never worry about them again. After getting a pinch of their hair, with the help of Machiavelli, my voodoo dolls gave them the pain they deserved for taking River away; may he rest in peace."

"May he rest in peace," everyone said.

"As your king, just like my father, I wish to humble myself in front of my people in hopes that I never look unfit to lead."

"We honor you, king," everyone said in unison, once again.

"But, as another brother leaves, a new one comes into our lives," Leonidas said as he pointed at Sapphire. "Our newest addition to the family is Sapphire. He has been nothing but a friend to all of us at Osiris and I'm so gracious to have him in my father's home. He's a sophisticated superior spell caster; some of you haven't seen one since my father's passing. He is very powerful and educated in the magical secrets that live in our world."

Patience gave Sapphire a pinch on the cheek as he tried to hold back a shy smile.

"Our community still remains protected under my surveillance...and of course the other three leaders. The Man might be able to shake our foundation, but they'll never be able to tear our kingdom down. Power to the people!"

"Power to the people!" everyone belted, with their fist rose as high as Leonidas' was.

"Now, is there anything that anyone else wants to

say, before Sapphire gives us a brilliant poem?"
Leonidas asked.

"Um, I have my numbers in about the money's we
pulled in from this year," said Alexandrite.

Sapphire snickered, that word, moneys was always
funny to him, especially when other adult's used it.

"Okay," Leonidas said as he took his seat.

"Um, it's great to be here," said Crystal, "that's all
I've got to say."

"Well, I want to announce something," said
Machiavelli as he stood up. "I wanted to let everyone
know that me and my girl just found out we're having
a baby."

Everyone irrupted into applause as Machiavelli
took his seat.

"Congrats, man," Leonidas said as Crystal slapped
hands with Machiavelli.

"Alright, well, awesome," said Leonidas. "I'm sure
she'll be just as bad as you are."

"Of course," said Patience. "His girl couldn't be
here tonight, Leonidas, she takes care of her
grandmother."

"I understand," Leonidas said. "Very good news,
man. Okay, great, now I would like to hear my boy,
Sapphire, give us a wonderful poem and then I'm
going downstairs to groove. I hear DJ Phunky
Phunker downstairs mixing them turntables."

Everyone chuckled as Sapphire got to his feet,
feeling his palms becoming sweaty as everyone looked
at him in silence.

Magenta smiled brighter than ever as if she was
about to watch him perform a piece that she had
helped him write.

"Well, I'm not used to a crowd this big, I usually perform these in front of my fam…but y'all are my fam, too, so, I guess it's not so different," Sapphire said.

"That's right, baby," said Patience.

"The poem is titled: This is 1996."

"Alright," said Neptune as she cackled.

"Let's go bro," said Napoleon with a smile.

And he read:

"The night has come and we've gathered here to feast, for work has been heavy and it has not been light. Bring in the candied yams, pot roast, roasted turkey, and greens. Set them down and enjoy each other in love. We will dine as a glorified people.

"Our hair will be curled, pressed and crimped. Our wheat colored boots will be on tight and our voices will be loud and proud throughout the night. But enjoy this time while you can, for it will be over quick. For the year is almost done, this is 1996.

"The king, Basquiat, has died and his crown no longer hangs over his head, we artist must carry this crown instead, for this is our rightful duty and we should be glad to adopt it. Our people's music is here and it's rapidly evolving. Let us keep it in our families, rich and full in volume, for this is 1996 and the sounds of black voices are emerging.

"They run up the streets and shatter windows. They fly through the air and stampede at the public. But we shouldn't quiet the voices, for they have been kept quiet so long and they should be heard now.

"When I die, if I do die in this year, I want you to give my lungs to the people without voices of their own. Keep my eyes but pass my vision down to the children – they'll know what to do with it. Give my hair back to my ancestors and most importantly give my tears to the people who caused them for this should be their property.

"Hold hands in a circle, sing hymns, dance, do whatever you can to keep the unity at hand, protect our men and keep our women from harm. Teach the children to believe in themselves and nurture the infant's in their cradles and secure the futures of the babies who are just ideas. Remember to love yourself for it gets lonely quick, for your own best friend could be a snake in 1996.

"Think on the good times as this year fades and keep your eyes from the current pain, for you are going to rise from the ashes once again. It's cold out so strap up in bundles. Make sure you getting paid so your stomach won't grumble. And Put on your warm scarf, cocoa butter and chapstick for it can get very cold-hearted in 1996."

Like his family back home, everyone clapped for him and Leonidas couldn't have smiled harder.

"That was mad dope, bruh," said Crystal, his eyes looking up and down at Sapphire who looked too shy to accept any compliments.

"How long have you been writing, man?" Alexandrite asked as she looked over at Sapphire.

"For about six years," said Sapphire, his eyes glowing. "I just love it – I live it."

"Oooooh, 'poetry in motion', that's straight fire, son," said Machiavelli with his hands clutched.

"You're really good," said Patience, "you're gonna have to write me something one day, young man."

"Sure," said Sapphire.

"Alright, let's pump, pump, pump it up!" said Othello as he compelled everyone to jump from their seats and make their way downstairs to a dance line that had already been made. Everyone stood on either side of the hall (some hanging out of their apartment rooms) as Othello led the way downstairs. A DJ, with huge earphones over his head, spun a funky beat as he twisted his turntables that were halfway outside of a middle apartment.

"Go, Othello, go, Othello," everyone chanted as Othello slid his way down the stairs to the second floor and did the snake, the bank head, the creep, the alf, a hip-hop version of the Charleston, and limboed his way out of the line.

Magenta vogu-ed her way through, causing two guys in cross colors to look very displeased.

Calypso did her best at the hill-toe with her long dress and after her was Leonidas and Machiavelli, who did the Kid-n-play before Napoleon did the electric slide. Sapphire was jerked by Neptune who made him do a half decent tango down the line and even dipped him, causing his black hat to hit the floor.

"Man, don't mess up the man's hat," Leonidas said as he picked up Sapphire's hat and handed it to him.

"Thanks, man," said Sapphire as he moved out of the way for Cirrus to moonwalk through while a few young girls on the left seemed heart struck by his moves.

"Aye, Sapphire," said Othello as he tugged on Sapphire's arm, "let's go in Machiavelli's room, he's got the game on."

"Alright, cool," said Sapphire as he laughed at

Crystal and Topaz, who was doing the Running Man.

The boys entered into Machiavelli's apartment, which was clustered with games, half opened snacks and full of, what appeared to be, scattered weed bags (which stunk in Sapphire's nostrils). A few people stood behind Sapphire and Othello who played their hearts out to fighting games while talking a generous amount of trash to one another.

Othello was good, but Sapphire was better.

"Move out the way, busta'," said Alexandrite as she shoved Othello over and took his controller.

"Man, quit pushing up on me, Alexandrite," said Othello as he got up to dust himself off.

"Hey, brotha'," Alexandrite said, before she knelt down beside Sapphire, ignoring Othello's words as she looked over at him. "Let me get you in a game, I ain't played this in a minute."

"Cool, Othello was losing anyway," said Sapphire. "I've never met a vampire before."

"Don't worry, my G, I won't bite," Alexandrite said as she looked over at Sapphire with a smile so large that it exposed her gold-plated fangs. "I feed on animal blood, and I already got my fix earlier, so I'm good. Now take this butt-whoopin', cuzz."

Alexandrite, her man and Machiavelli's big cousin all lost to Sapphire and as he did a victory dance, Neptune rushed in the room and announced, "hey, everyone, Leonidas and Calypso are about to do the Transformation dance."

"Oh, snap, yo'," said Othello as he rushed out of Machiavelli's room that had been overcrowded with all of his cousins who wanted to play Sapphire.

"Come on, Sapphire, you've got to see this. They

only do it once a year!"

"What, what are you talking about?" Sapphire asked as he ran after Othello who squeeze through a mob of dancers.

As he pushed for a clearer view of outside, Othello educated Sapphire on the Transformation Dance.

"Every year, Leonidas and Calypso do a dance where they channel each other's strength and use it to shapeshift."

"Whoa," said Sapphire as he stood by Napoleon who was behind Neptune.

"See, look," said Othello as everyone beheld Leonidas and Calypso with their palms touching, moving in a circle as they looked each other in the eyes.

Everyone that had formed a circle around them clapped and chanted with smiles on their faces, Magenta looking halfway drunk or maybe even high as she clapped the loudest, and offbeat.

"His mom and dad used to do this," said Othello as Sapphire looked around to see that everyone had rushed outside. "It's a very strong, very powerful voodoo transformation spell. Leonidas said that Osiris could shapeshift whenever he wanted, but he let his wife channel his power and shapeshift, too."

"It's beautiful," said Neptune as she put her hands together as if to pray.

"Channeling is hard to do," said Cirrus as he walked up behind Sapphire. "Leonidas learned from his pops and taught Calypso...but he just can't seem to get us to do it. He says we just need more years of practice like he –"

"Whoa!" said Sapphire as Leonidas no longer was

171

his tall frame but an alligator with dark green skin and teeth that looked like razors. When he had transformed it had happened so fast as if he was bending and twisting and then – suddenly he was an entirely different shape. A scaly beast that ran up at Nicoleto, who jerked back a few feet with fright in his eyes, causing everyone to laugh.

"Ha, Nicoleto, you gone be alright foo'," said Machiavelli who sat on his black motorcycle that had been right next to a barrel with a bright churning flame inside.

"Let's go, Calypso," said Neptune as Leonidas had resumed his rightful position and smiled at Calypso with jeering eyes.

Calypso touched hands with Leonidas, her eyes full of ambition, as she became a ferocious wolf with an all-white fur and the most beautiful blue eyes Sapphire had seen. She pranced around delicately and licked at Othello's face that had gotten dangerously close for a better view.

After Calypso dashed into her natural form, Leonidas became Othello, stunningly identical, with the same smile, baggy jeans, tank and cornrows. Othello scoffed as if he had been told a very dramatic bit of news and the duplicate version of himself did the snake but not nearly as good as he could.

Calypso became a sassy, pink flamingo on one leg and then – with a great roar – Leonidas burst into a lion with golden mane and teeth that could tear out a man's flesh in seconds. Everyone stood back this time; no one was brave enough to stand in the presence of Leonidas in this tremendous form. He marched around slowly and eyed everyone as Calypso stood with no fear in her eyes, her face smirking as everyone else looked terrified, especially Sapphire and Othello.

But quickly – before Leonidas could roar again, Calypso touched his mane, drew from his strength and became a blue dragon with four sharp wings, a long, pointed tail and blue whiskers emerging from her face. At least two people fainted, Sapphire's skin sprouted with goosebumps and Othello screamed in satisfaction. In such a large figure, Calypso did not fly high but swirled around in a majestic circle around Leonidas who bellowed, "show off!"

And after that, Calypso had become her normal self, resting on the concrete on her knees with her right hand on her stomach.

Everyone clapped as loud as they could, Patience helped Calypso to her feet and Leonidas humbly announced that she had won this time.

"Man, I love the Magicians," said Crystal as he stood behind Cirrus, his shoulder resting on the doorway.

"We're spectacular, huh?" said Othello as he turned around to slap hands with Crystal.

"Sho' is," said Crystal as he looked over at Sapphire. "Hey, you, what's yo' name again?"

"Me?" Sapphire asked as he turned behind himself to look at Crystal.

"Yeah," said Crystal, his eyes on Sapphire.

"My name is Sapphire."

"Well, why don't you two brotha's come ride with me and the boys? We just gone cruise for a minute, my G, you down?"

"Ride?" Sapphire asked, his throat closing up.

"Yeah, ride."

"Like, motorcycles?" Sapphire said as he looked over to a standing line up of black motorcycles that rested beside Machiavelli.

"Nah, duh?" said Othello, as he looked at Sapphire. "I wanna go, man, come on let's do it."

"Leonidas, Othello's about to go riding with Crystal and Machiavelli," said Calypso as she sat on the hood of a car with Magenta and Patience.

"Snitch," spat Othello.

"I don't know, Othello," said Leonidas as he looked over at the boys while pausing his conversation with Pierre, who was smoking a cigar.

"Please, please, please, please," said Othello as he made the ugliest face he could to prove how desperate he was.

"Come on, Leonidas, I'll let him ride with me," said Cirrus. "I'll go slow."

"Yeah, Leonidas, we'll cruise," said Machiavelli as he revved up his own motorcycle engine.

"Y'all dudes don't be wearing no helmets though," said Leonidas. "I don't know."

"Whatever I break, Sapphire can heal with his magic," said Othello.

"Sapphire, you going?" Leonidas asked.

"Man, I'm only a year younger than him, I should be able to make my own decisions," Othello said.

"If Sapphire goes you can go, but, only because I know he could heal you," Leonidas said.

"You going, Sapphire, right?" Othello asked as he looked at Sapphire with pleading eyes.

At first, a big no was about to emerge, but Sapphire didn't want to spoil the night. Othello was his best bud, he didn't want to disappoint him and most of all he couldn't look wimpy in front of everyone by refusing to go ride a motorcycle.

"Yeah, I'm going," Sapphire said as he felt his stomach turn to ice.

"I'm going, man."

"Cool, you can go, Bubby," said Leonidas as he winked at Othello, causing everyone to laugh.

"Ew, I hate when he calls me that," Othello said as he walked off with Cirrus, who started his motorcycle.

"I'm coming, too," said Neptune as she brushed against Topaz. "Can I ride with you ?"

"Um, sure," said Topaz as he zipped up his brown, leather jacket.

"You can ride with me," said Crystal as he slapped hands with Sapphire, the smell of cigarettes and strong soap slipping off his body, "Machiavelli don't like nobody riding with him.

"Okay," whispered Sapphire as he handed his hat to Leonidas who had approached them.

"Be safe with my boys," said Leonidas as he looked at Crystal. "I'm serious, brotha'."

"It's all good, Leonidas," said Crystal as he revved up his engine while Sapphire boarded behind, placing his feet on the footrest. "Your boys are in good hands."

"I don't see how y'all ride them thangs," said Alexandrite as she leaned against the steps that led to the front door. "I'd be scared I was gone fall, huh daddy?"

"Mmmhmm," Aristotle said

"Y'all be careful with them boys," said Patience.

"Ma, we got it," said Machiavelli, and with a loud

grumble, Crystal and Sapphire led off the pack with Othello on Cirrus's bike, Neptune on Crystals and Napoleon and Machiavelli on both sides of them.

The cool air, the bumpy exit and the chilling feeling of riding a motorcycle all made Sapphire's head hurt, but the fact that Crystal was cruising made him feel ensured that he wouldn't suffer a deadly accident tonight.

"Hold on to me, man," said Crystal as he rode off, the other's on the sides of him like wings on an angel.

"Okay," Sapphire whispered as he tried to hold his breath. Did these guys always ride without helmets, he thought.

He gripped around Crystal's waist and tried not to shiver too wildly, as to hide the fact that he was terrified of this experience.

Othello looked overjoyed, his eye's squinting as he clutched on to Cirrus. Neptune looked very happy with the state she was in as she not only gripped Topaz very tightly but seemed to be rubbing on his chest and arms as they rode along.

A rush of excitement crept up in Sapphire's body as he started to like his ride. He had done many new things, scary things, ever since leaving home, but this seemed like it came with the least amount of consequences.

They drove through a park and passed a series of closed shopping buildings with glass windows that reflected their appearances. Sapphire could see himself, never had he thought that he would ride a motorcycle, and definitely not at twenty. He had shattered his father's car window, burned down a school and now he was riding a motorcycle, was he becoming a rebel or was he already one?

"CIRCLE FORMATION!" roared Crystal as the other riders grouped together in an empty parking lot, everyone slowing down so that they could make a circle of themselves; chasing one another's tail ends.

"Cooool!" Othello screamed as Sapphire couldn't help but smile because of how awesome the riders were. After breaking out, Crystal led again, but Machiavelli and Topaz had sped up so that they looked like a capital M.

"Nice," said Crystal.

Neptune smirked as Topaz tipped up his front tire to ride off just the back for a moment, Othello's eyes lighting up at the sight.

"Sick, bruh," said Crystal as Sapphire feared that he would do the same thing and moments later realized Crystal was into outdoing his older brother after he tipped up his back tire and rode on the front even longer, Sapphire's cheek smoothed into the back of his leather jacket.

"Can we do one?" Othello asked as he pulled on Cirrus's arm.

"No, I'm not doing no stunts with you on," said Cirrus. "I don't wanna risk nothing."

"You just can't do none," said Othello, with a smirk as everyone noticed Crystal was leading the pack towards what looked like an old, stone Catholic church with a tall steeple and two large pillars on either side.

"Not the church, again?" said Machiavelli as he and the rest of the riders stopped their bikes and rested in front of the tall, red doors of the church.

"Chill, yo'," said Crystal, I've got to say a prayer

here, I ain't been in a minute."

"It's been two weeks," said Topaz as he walked up to Crystal, who had let out the kickstand of his motorcycle so that Sapphire could get off.

"You go to church?" Othello asked as he looked at Crystal, who took out a cigarette and lit it.

"Yup," Crystal said. "My grandmother used to come get us and take us here, when we were kids." Crystal looked up at the top of the church that had a wooden sign that read: If God Be For Us, Who Can Be Against Us?

"She stopped taking us on Sundays when she died...in our teens," Topaz said as he stood just a little bit higher, besides Crystal.

"We come here, to remember her, and say a prayer like she did, that God will be forgiving of us. Cause we all need it."

Forgiveness: a word Sapphire had been hearing quite often after all of his tragedies. The question was, who needed it more, the people he had hurt or himself, for all the damage he had done as well. Burning a school up was now on his timeline, he didn't just bust his father's window but he abandoned his mother in her time of distress, magically pushed his father into a wall and kept Seraphina and Cerberus as his captives; against their will. But could God forgive him, was God even real? Sapphire never knew a lot about God and had heard many different things, many different opinions, but was never sure which one to grasp.

"Last time, it took me forever to pick this stupid lock, I figured you could do it easily with your...magic," Crystal said as he looked at Sapphire.

"Could you, please."

"Um, sure, yeah," said Sapphire.

I'm breaking into a church now, how bad can I get, Sapphire asked as he walked up to the red doors of the church. He looked behind himself and couldn't see anyone insight that might report them for breaking in, the church was sort of out of eye view, and two abandoned homes by it assured him that no one would be driving by any time soon, or at least he hoped.

"I haven't used this spell in a while so I don't know if it'll work, cause I might not get the incantation right," Sapphire said as he moved his hands towards the door's handles. "Um, uh, Perezma Ano Tora."

"Yes," said Othello as the doors of the church opened with a crack.

"Thank you so much," said Crystal as he hugged Sapphire before he could say that it was okay. "We love you magicians, man. I don't know what we would do without y'all. Come on Topaz, say a prayer with me."

"Aight," said Topaz as he walked in with Crystal, before turning to say, "y'all all can come in if you want...and pray with us. Or just come in to get out of the cold and get warm."

"I'll take the warmth," said Neptune as she entered into the church with everyone else including Sapphire who entered in last to close the doors behind himself.

Inside the church were two long immaculate rows of caramel pews to the left and to the right. Tall, stained glass windows of all sorts of colors, the beautifully carved arches of the ceiling and the golden altar in front all were food for the architectural soul that Sapphire possessed. Machiavelli, Cirrus and Napoleon all sat down at the back pews as Crystal and Topaz knelt at the very front to pray.

It was dim inside, and so Sapphire lifted up his hands and about twelve tiny orbs of light appeared and flew up into the air, glowing as they grew. The light orbs looked like stars, bright enough to light a room individually. They each grew to be about the size of a globe and floated near the massive ceiling of the church.

"Beautiful," Neptune whispered as she gazed up at the lights that made all the gold in the church shimmer.

"I can do it too," said Othello as he lifted up his hands and said, "Lampsionu," a short bud of light shooting up from his hand and falling down in glittering dust. Cirrus snickered.

"Keep practicing that incantation, the more you do, you won't even need to say words, homie," said Sapphire as he gripped Othello's shoulder.

"I've got to do it," said Crystal as he walked away from his brother who had tried to grab him.

"No, Crystal, you cannot play that thing!" said Topaz, his eyes burning into Crystal's face. "Somebody is gone hear you, dude. Let's go."

"I've got to, grandma played here, man. I've got to touch them keys."

"You can play it when we come during church, but not now."

"You ain't my daddy," said Crystal as he sprinted off to walk up the right side of the winged stair case that led to a pipe organ on a balcony.

"Just don't be forever," said Topaz as he looked up at Crystal who had begun to play soft music on the four-decker organ. The full moon could be seen through a large rose-colored window that was above the organ and it attracted Sapphire as he walked up the steps to get a closer experience of Crystal's melodies.

"Stop running around this church boy," said Topaz, who mean mugged Othello as he ran around the pews, avoiding a very angry Cirrus who was trying to snatch him up. "Chill out, Cirrus."

"Well, tell this little dude to stop pulling my dreads before I beat the breaks off him."

Napoleon raised his hand and Othello's left and right shoelaces tied themselves together, making him fall. Everyone bellowed in laughter, especially Cirrus.

"Y'all play too much," said Sapphire as he turned over to see Othello get up with what looked like a small, ashy mark on his arm; he looked furious.

"You cool, Othello," said Topaz as he rested on the winged steps, looking down on the boys while they threw insults at each other.

"I'm good," said Othello as he shrugged off his aggression, rolling his eyes after seeing that Neptune couldn't stop herself from laughing.

"Man, y'all gotta' get out of this church, before y'all break some stuff, man...come upstairs with me, I wanna show y'all this cool view of the east tower roof, it's crazy."

"I'm down," said Napoleon.

"Beats sittin' in here," said Neptune.

"Cool, cool, let's go," said Othello as he walked out with Crystal, who led everyone up a spiral staircase near the entrance of the church.

"We on the roof, Crystal, when you done, boy!" said Machiavelli as he looked up at the organ balcony.

"Aight, bruh," said Crystal, his fingers still tickling the keys, his eyes watching them carefully as a tiny speck of a tear fell from his eye.

"Are you...you...okay?" said Sapphire as he leaned over Crystal's left shoulder.

"I just...I wanted to remember her, by playing the same organ she used to play," Crystal said as he continued to play. "I didn't know I'd be shedding no tears, B." He smiled, turning to Sapphire, "I just... it's a lot I go through...the family business...these other janky gangs hatin' on our hustle and the pigs...and through all this, I don't have her here."

Sapphire couldn't believe his eyes, a thug – a drug dealer who appeared to have a tough exterior was shedding it to reveal his soft side; his emotions. With a tear, Crystal gave Sapphire the reason to understand that everybody, including the leaders of criminal gangs, had feelings and even wanted to express them.

"I mean, my dad's here, and my brother – but ain't nothing like your grandma, man," Crystal said, as the lights from above revealed his smooth, light skin when he lifted his head high. "And my ma, she don't agree with the whole drug thing, that's why her and my dad never got along; but...but my grandma never judged...even when she found out I was following after pops' footsteps."

Why he was opening up to him, Sapphire wondered what he had that made Crystal feel as if he could start telling him his personal life. Sapphire had been told that he had a great personality and a soothing voice but maybe it was the fact that no one else had bothered to ask.

"I love my dad, man, but sometimes, I wonder how long I'm gone keep up the business. Some days I just stay in it for the money...cause we sho' bring in a lot, but I want a family of my own, a wife...little girl; and I don't know if I want her to have the family inheritance. My dad would probably hate me if I left the business...he can be very closed minded sometimes."

"Yeah, my dad too," said Sapphire.

"You like your pops?"

"Well, no, not right now," Sapphire said as he turned to look over the organ balcony, getting a closer look at the craftsmanship that went into the mighty arches.

"Not right now?" Crystal asked.

"Yeah, he really is on my bad side," Sapphire said. "He...he...I love him, don't get me wrong —"

"Okay."

"But he hurt me and my mom. He cheated on her...and tore our family apart. My mother was a dear to him...hard working devoted wife, but he couldn't see how valuable she was. Not...not until she said DIVORCE, no."

"Divorce, foreal?"

Sapphire walked back over to Crystal as he got up from the organ.

"Now, I probably will never have my family together for Thanksgiving, ever again," he said. "Who knew that just last month's Thanksgiving was going to be the last with my mom and dad?"

Crystal looked at him with sincere eyes, and then

he hugged Sapphire, and with a squeeze; it was as if he was trying to absorb some of that superior power, enough of it at least to get through life for another month. But Crystal was a non-magical man, he couldn't channel, he couldn't absorb, all he could do was offer Sapphire something that he needed at this hour, and that was his compassion in the form of a hug.

"Thanks," said Sapphire, breaking away.

"I hope everything works out, man," Crystal said. "Hey...let's go upstairs with everybody, the view is really cool."

"Alright," said Sapphire as he waved his hands at the orbs of light, and they shrunk into one whole ball of light that rested above his hand.

As they walked out of a rusted door that led out to the flat, concrete roof of the tower, Sapphire could see that everyone was getting a great view of the city and all its many lights. Neptune was hugged up with Topaz, Machiavelli smoked a cigarette, and Napoleon and Cirrus stood by Othello who was doing very elegant ballet moves, his arms stretched and his legs spinning as he balanced on the toe of his white sneakers.

"I didn't know you knew ballet," Sapphire breathed as Othello held his balance on one foot, his arms stretched out. "Yeah," he said, "I'm not so good at it, my dance partner at my school was way better than me. I'm just doing everything I saw her do."

"Well, it's magnificent," said Sapphire as he looked over the stone wall of the tower.

"Thanks, man," Othello said as he joined Sapphire in the view.

"I know you said you like architecture and sculpting and stuff...check out these angels up here."

Sapphire turned to his right and saw a statue of an angel, in the corner; his stone wings stretching out as if he was about to fly away any second. His body was clothed in a paved stone tunic that revealed half of his muscular frame.

"I can just see the artist taking his time on this," Sapphire said, as he looked over at Othello who glanced back at the statue.

"Yeah," said Othello as he stretched out his arms, "look at those wings, cool. Oooooh if I could just fly, that'd be so awesome. I bet angels have a field day in heaven, flying around on those big wings."

Sapphire looked over at the angel again and then around at everyone else, "let's do it."

"What?" Othello asked.

"Let's do it, let's fly –"

"You want to FLY? Now?" Othello asked.

"Fly?" said Napoleon as he overheard the boys' conversation. "Who's flyin'?"

"We are, right now, everyone is," said Sapphire as he backed away from Othello. "Everyone give yourself room –"

"I don't know about this, Sapphire," said Cirrus. "None of us are as powerful as you –"

"And some of us can barely levitate a pot," said Neptune as she winked at Othello.

"What if one of us falls?" Othello asked.

"Then I'll catch you – I'm a superior aren't I?" Sapphire asked, his eyes squinting. "Come on, we can do this. You all haven't been so successful at your spells before, cause you don't work them, and you

185

don't work them cause you don't believe in your magic. All things are possible if you believe."

"I don't know, Sapphire," breathed Neptune as she looked over at Napoleon and Cirrus, who looked just as nervous as Othello.

"We are going to do this," Sapphire demanded. "Let's end this night on a wild note. If anyone feels like they're losing control call my name and I'll hold you up. My power, that flows through me is strong, I know what I'm capable of. I'll even help you all up first, but we've got to do it, guys...."

"Aight, B," said Cirrus as he ran his fingers through his dreadlocks.

"Coo, I'm down," said Othello.

"Well, me and the non-magicians are gonna be safe on the ground," said Topaz as he smirked over at Machiavelli. "Come on guys."

"I wanna fly," said Crystal as he approached Sapphire, his eyes reflecting the gleam of the moon. "Can I fly...can you make me fly?"

"Crystal, no. Come down with us."

"No, no...I wanna fly too, Sapphire's got me," said Crystal.

"I'll lift you up, man," said Sapphire. "Just hold on to my shoulders and I'll take you up with me."

"Bet," said Crystal, as Topaz scoffed and walked downstairs with Machiavelli.

Everyone stood across from each other, giving one another space, as Sapphire instructed.

"I can do this," Othello whispered as he stretched out his arms.

"That's right, believe you can," said Sapphire, his face brushed by the cool wind from the north.

"Everyone focus on your body; focus on the direction you want it to go. Stretch your arms out wide to balance your own body and think up."

"Think up," Othello whispered.

"Okay," said Neptune, her eyes closed.

"Crystal, hold on to me," Sapphire said, "Hold on to me."

"Okay, bro," said Crystal as he gripped onto Sapphire's shoulders.

"Everyone, on the count of three," yelled Sapphire. "One...two (he took a deep swallow) three!"

With no hesitation, Sapphire lifted his body from the stone roof under his feet. Crystal, without adding any weight to him, levitated along with him, his eyes wide opened as he couldn't believe that he was in the air without any strings or chords, but by magic.

Then, Cirrus – then Neptune – and Napoleon. One by one, they all floated up. Othello, with his eyes shut tight, had lifted off last, his cheeks red, his arm muscles straining.

The six, all in formation, were five feet from the stone roof, the wind gusting through their hair, the night chill compelling them to come down and be warm downstairs, but, the rush of flying begging them to go even higher.

"Wicked, yo'!" Crystal said as he looked down at Machiavelli and Topaz, who rested on their motorcycles, scoffing as they watched the magicians slowly float from over the church tower.

"Whhooooohooooo," bellowed Napoleon as he swooshed around in circles. "If you told me I'd be doing this tonight I wouldn't believe you man...."

"Everyone is doing beautiful, beautiful," said Sapphire. "Now, see if you can keep up."

Sapphire grinned as he floated off east, almost dashing away as the other's followed behind. His dreadlocks slapped against Crystal's face as he tried to see where he was going. With a smirk, Sapphire flew over clouds, and under clotheslines.

"Hey," said Neptune as she soared beside Sapphire, "not everyone is as excepting of our powers as the non-magicians back home are. We can't be seen, Sapphire."

"I know, I know," said Sapphire as he turned back to see that Othello was still floating behind. He could see that he was beginning to lower, even more than the rest, so he lifted him higher, not feeling an inch of power leave his body.

"Let's turn around," said Napoleon.

"Yeah, we got to get back before Machiavelli and Crystal think we're flying south for the winter," goofed Cirrus as Othello did circle flips in midair, his mouth unable to calm his wide smile.

"Aight, no prob," said Sapphire as he flew along with the others, Crystal still on his back, now floating above him as he glided like an eagle.

A little black girl, and a boy smaller than her, looked out of their apartment window and they awed in wonder as Sapphire winked at them while soaring past their view.

16 DEATH

"Get out!" roared Cirrus as he walked into his room to see that Sapphire and Othello were playing on his game. The boys had managed to sneak in with the help of their magic, and now, they had to face his wrath, and he looked already bothered with his day.

"I'm gone kill y'all," Cirrus said as he stood blocking his door.

"Skoniori," Sapphire yelled as he opened his hand and a gust of glittery confetti burst out and bombarded Cirrus's face. He spat and leaned against the hall as Sapphire sprung up with Othello and they ran out of the room.

"Napoleon! Get 'em!" Cirrus yelled as Napoleon jumped out from his room in just his leather pants, his arms open as to intercept, but, failed when Othello grabbed Sapphire's hand and disappeared into a puff of black smoke, only to reappear behind him on the back steps.

He had done it, Napoleon almost choked, and Cirrus, he couldn't believe what Othello had just done either.

"Did you, did you just...." Napoleon was lost for words as he gazed at Othello whose eyes were wide open.

"Nah, man, no way, that was Sapphire," said

Othello.

"I…didn't teleport, Othello, you did," Sapphire said as he looked at Othello. "You did that."

"No. I did?"

"If I wasn't so mad I'd congratulate you, dumbo," said Cirrus as he walked up by Napoleon, his leather jacket covered in red, yellow, pink and bright blue paper confetti scraps. They were everywhere, especially in his hair.

"Oooooh, I'm hungry," said Neptune as she stretched out to see what everyone was discussing, her outfit from yesterday still on, her black eyeliner smudged. "What are you goofballs talking about," she asked.

"Othello just teleported," Napoleon said as he turned to Neptune, noticing Topaz walk out of her room.

"Oh, cool," said Neptune as she leaned against her wall. "What's that all over Cirrus?"

"Forget me, who's that leaving your room?" Cirrus asked sarcastically, as Topaz grinned while kissing Neptune goodbye. "You know there's no non-magical peeps that can stay overnight, you breaking Leonidas's rules."

"Well, I never heard him say that," said Neptune.

"Say what?" Leonidas asked as he walked down the stairs from his room in a white T, baggy jeans and a long necklace of red feathers.

"Nothing," Neptune smirked as Leonidas picked at the confetti in Cirrus's hair.

"You need to let me wash your hair, my dude," said Leonidas as he frowned down. "You had a rough night, Cirrus?"

"Man, I'm going back to my room," said Cirrus as

he stormed off to his room while Sapphire and Othello snickered.

"Well, I'm hungry and I don't smell breakfast, sooooo, that means I'm cooking," said Leonidas.

"Cool, your food never takes as long as Calypso's," said Othello as he walked downstairs with everyone who followed after Leonidas.

After the voodoo king made grilled egg sandwiches (with the help of Sapphire and Othello) he sat down to share with everyone at the dining table in the hall. Cirrus had come down dressed in a red leather jacket and a Nirvana tank top that Napoleon had given him and sat by Sapphire.

"Calypso still isn't up," Othello said while chomping on his sandwich. "Maybe she's still weak from all that transformation magic last night.

"I'll go see what's taking her," said Neptune as she walked upstairs to the second floor.

Then, as she came back down, moments later, her face was blank; she blinked and then sat down on Leonidas's right. "She was crying," she said, as she rested her chin on her palm.

"Crying?" Leonidas asked. "Crying...really?"

"Yeah," Neptune whispered.

Sapphire looked around, was this a normal thing for Calypso to cry in the mornings or was this the first time they had heard about it?

"She's...she probably had a bad dream about the world ending or some apocalypse that will happen in one hundred years," said Leonidas as he saw the stillness on everyone's face. "Her visions...they just come...unexpectedly. She probably just needs about a day by herself. Poor thing. I'll check on her, tonight."

"Good...she was sobbing like a baby," said

Neptune.

Leonidas cleared his throat, "let's just go around the table and get out anything we need to, whatever's on our chest, let's get it off."

"Well, I'm happy to share that my job is going great," said Neptune. "And I'm so glad that Sapphire taught us to fly yesterday (Sapphire smiled) it was great, really."

"Yeah, I was so shocked when Calypso had told me that you guys were gonna do that," Leonidas said with a wide grin. "What would we do without our beloved Sapphire."

"Die of boredom," said Othello.

"Oh, shut up," said Cirrus. "You ain't entertained until you're getting on somebody nerve – or breaking into my room."

"Sorry, dude, dang," said Othello.

"You sharing today, Cirrus?" Leonidas asked with a smirk.

"Uh, man, whatever," said Cirrus, his hands stretched out on the table. "I'm thinking bout making peace with my brother. I ain't seen him since he kicked me out – before trying to shoot me over some old chic we use to fight over...."

"That's good," said Leonidas.

"I keep hearing everybody talk about forgiveness, so, I take that as a sign that I need to."

"Yeah...."

"That's it, bruh."

"Okay," said Leonidas. "Sapphire?"

"I had a great time last night, with everyone," Sapphire said. "And I hope to be a part of many more Brethren Gatherings."

"Cool," said Leonidas as he could sense that

Sapphire didn't wish to say more. "My boy, Othello?"

"I called my mom's yesterday," said Othello. "We still ain't seeing eye to eye on her situation with her dude, but (he looked down) it's all good. I'm done."

"Thank you for your share," said Leonidas.

"Before I head off to work," said Napoleon, "I just want to say, Sapphire, you da' man for getting us to fly last night," said Napoleon. "And, uh, I love everybody around here."

"And, I love everybody as well," said Leonidas. "And that's my share."

"Coo'," said Cirrus as he got up from the table, shoving at Othello's head.

"Stop buggin', yo'," said Othello. "Aye, Leonidas can we have some cheddar to go shopping with? Sapphire wanted to take me to 5th avenue to go kick it, but I'm dead broke."

"Aight, here, bruh," said Leonidas as he reached in his pocket and handed Othello two hundred dollars. "Don't spend it all on candy and dirty magazines, boy."

"Thanks, Leonidas, you da' beez-neez," Othello said as he walked upstairs to grab his jacket.

"Watch em, Sapphire," said Leonidas as he stood up, "you know that boy can be a loose cannon."

"Aight," said Sapphire as he went upstairs to change into a warmer outfit, which consisted of a blue and black striped sweater and ripped jeans.

He placed his wide-brimmed, black fedora on his dreadlocks that he had put in a ponytail and met Othello in his room that still had a strong scent of old socks.

"We're teleporting to 5th avenue," he said.

"Foreal!" Othello asked as he put on a grey

hoodie. "That stuff is weird, B. But I like it."

"Yeah, I don't, but I'm not riding no subway cause they're creepy, and I don't feel like busing there, it be too many musty hobos on there always panhandling."

"Aye, brotha' man, you got change for a beer," Othello mocked as Sapphire snickered.

"Here, grab ahold of my hand, Othello," he said as Othello followed his orders. "We're going a little further than down the hall, so it might feel even weirder but –"

"It's cool, I'm ready," said Othello with his eyes closed.

"Alright," said Sapphire, blinking as he concentrated on an alley between an arcade and a shoe store that he frequently visited.

Unlike before, it didn't take much of a push, the boys vanished, felt as if they were on a roller coaster off its hinges and then appeared in a brick alleyway, near a smelly dumpster.

It was getting colder out and December wasn't being gentle to New Yorkers anymore. The chill of the city was biting with all its teeth, but that didn't stop Sapphire and Othello from having a good time. The boy's, played at a two-story arcade, acted like children at a toy store and Othello collected money in Sapphire's hat as he performed his newest moves on a very busy street; also doing his ballet dances that Sapphire requested. Othello was taken to go ice skating at the Rockefeller skate rink, where Sapphire's own dad would take him every year. There, as he and Othello took in the view of the grand Christmas tree, he thought of his father and even developed a yearning for him. He was beginning to miss Leander, more than he wanted to. The boys had passed by a large hotel building and gazed at a black limousine.

"Oooooh, that mug is stretched, yo'," said Othello, wonder in his eyes.

"Sho' is," said Sapphire.

"I ain't ever got in one before," Othello said. "Have you?"

"Yeah, my dad used to drive for a limo company a few years back, and used to always let me ride in them."

The boys stood a foot away from the hotel entrance and watched as the driver, with a black flat cap and suit, got out to open the back door.

"Hey, sir, excuse me," said Othello as he walked up to the driver.

"What?" breathed the driver in an irritated tone.

"Can me and my friend ride around the block?"

"Yeah," said Sapphire as he walked up beside Othello. "Can we, please?"

"No," the driver said.

"Aw, come on, my boy here ain't ever got to ride in one," said Sapphire as he put his arm over Othello's shoulder's, "come on. Can we at least look inside –?"

"Nope, every day I come here at 2:00 pm to pick up someone far more important than you two boogers, and I don't do it for free, now scram."

"Whatever." Sapphire shrugged and beckoned for Othello to pay a visit to the Metropolitan Museum of Art.

The boys feasted their eye's on the fine Egyptian art, with its golden history, Greece's sculptures and new modern paintings that had been added to an exhibit.

"Paintings are the minds words that can't be

uttered by the mouth," Sapphire said as he and Othello examined a large oil painting of the solar system and all its beautiful features.

After a lesson on classical Chinese sculpting and a Haiku demonstration in a poetry session, the boys shopped for shoes at a three-story mall. Wheat boots were definitely in style around New York, no matter what borough one came from, and Sapphire and Othello couldn't wait to change into there's before they left the store. Before leaving the block that the store sat on, a police car bleeped and an officer with brownish blond hair beckoned for them to stop.

With his partner, a bald pale man, the officer got out and commanded that the boys put down their shoe bags and put their hands on the wall.

"What – why?" Sapphire asked as he was frisked by the leading officer, who had a very raspy voice, his blue eyes piercing the back of his neck.

"Shut up and do what I say," the officer said. "Giuseppe, search the other boy. You two hooligans just couldn't let these hard-working store workers have peace, huh?"

"Get off me, man!" Othello yelled as the bald officer named Giuseppe forced his face against the cold brick, his cheek brushing against its rough surface.

"Calm down, Othello," said Sapphire. "We ain't did nothing wrong. I demand your license number and your name officer–"

"My name's Bartholomew, boy, but you too young man can call me Sir, understood."

"We got a call that two black boys stole from this shoe store, you boys got a receipt?" Giuseppe asked.

"I'm a grown man, not a boy," said Sapphire.

"And our receipts are in my bags."

"We ain't take nothing – y'all just don't want to see two black men with they own money," Othello barked.

"Watch your stankin' mouth, punk, before we bust it open," Bartholomew said.

Everyone who walked past didn't question the cops for how forceful they were with Othello and Sapphire, and according to Sapphire they probably just thought it was a normal thing to see black men in a cops hold. Sapphire had never been arrested or searched; this was all new to him.

"Check our bags," said Sapphire as Giuseppe looked inside the shoe bags, grabbing two receipts out.

"You got the wrong guys," said Othello.

"It's all here," said Giuseppe, who looked very irritated with the way Othello mean mugged him. "They're good, Bartholomew."

Sapphire was released from Bartholomew's grip around his shoulders and he picked up his bag and dusted off Othello's cheek.

"Are you all supposed to be this rough?" Sapphire questioned.

"Watch your mouth, little brown boy," said Bartholomew, who looked heated that he couldn't find any dirt on the boys. "Let's get out of here Giuseppe before I hurt one of these kids...before they just hurt themselves anyway. Probably stole the little money they got now."

As the cops walked away to their vehicle, Othello, with his nostrils flared yelled out, "go eat a donut you racist crackers!"

They stopped. Sapphire turned to Othello.

Bartholomew turned around with a smirk.

"I'ma remember your face, little black boy, I'm gone get you," Bartholomew whispered, his finger pointing at Othello as if to penetrate him with fear. But Othello didn't budge as the cops sped away.

"You okay, man," Sapphire asked as he could see a tear fall down Othello's face. "It's alright…you okay (he placed his arm around him as he walked him back to the arcade). It's cool, they was just some racist pigs, B."

"I shoulda' hit him dead in his jaw," said Othello, his breathing heavy.

"I know…I know you mad, bruh. They ain't nothing…just brush 'em off, Othello. Come on, let's go back to the arcade, I know you wanna go back."

The idea of playing games made Othello smile, but in his heart he felt a brush of sadness, racism plucked at his heartstrings and compelled him to be angry.

It wasn't fair to him.

The boys sat on the arcade steps after beating almost everyone in a Street Fighter tournament.

Sapphire was munching on a bag of chips and Othello was whistling at almost every girl that walked in the arcade, but none of them paid him any mind.

"These chica's acting like they don't see me, man," said Othello.

"Probably cause they too busy looking at me," Sapphire giggled as he shoved at Othello's arm.

"Man, whatever, you probably right tho', I'm not that good looking to be real."

"Oh, whatever, no way," said Sapphire. "Yes, you are."

"Man, dats hard to believe, yo'. Especially when ya moms boyfriend calls you ugly every chance he gets."

Othello put his head down as Sapphire patted his back.

"He said that to you...he called you ugly?" Sapphire asked. "That's not true, Othello, and you know what...we gone send a hex his way when we get back home. Yeah, make his teeth fall out or give him an extra eye on his forehead – since he can't see clearly."

"I really hate him, yo'," said Othello. "He came into our lives and tore our family apart and shoved himself right in the middle. First, he was nice but then I realized he was just a no good chump like my daddy. And I barely knew him."

"Huh, well, I'm sorry to hear that, Othello. But, if it makes you feel any better, I think you could get any girl if you just walk up to her yourself." Sapphire balled up his chip bag and threw it at Othello while standing up. "Just say hey pretty ladies my name is Othello. I can dance and I'm all that and a bag of...."

Othello looked up to see that Sapphire wasn't speaking. He looked as if he had just been pierced with a knife; his eyes still, his speech paused.

Everything happened so fast he did understand what was going on.

He couldn't perceive.

He couldn't believe.

In front of him, standing in a red coat, tan skirt and burgundy boots was Seraphina, she looked at Sapphire as he stood still, not moving a muscle. He looked at her with eyes that could tell stories he could never finish. He said so much in his stair: I love you, I can't stand you, I don't want to be bothered – why are you here?

Her eyes spoke of regret, that hadn't changed, she

still looked sorry, but sadder than ever before.

"Let's go, Othello," Sapphire said as he didn't take his eyes of the woman that had shattered his heart, "I'm ready to go home."

Othello didn't hesitate, nor did he question Sapphire as they walked away from Seraphina's view, back to the alleyway where they had teleported to.

The boys stood in the center of the dim alleyway and checked for people walking by. Just when they had touched hands someone entered in, his eyes full of anger, his hand gripping his gun, his mouth clenched.

"I told you I was gone get you for that smart mouth, little black filth," Bartholomew said as he looked at Othello, his voice causing them to turn around in a startle.

They were trapped.

Cornered.

Who could see that they were in a jam?

He was holding his gun straight at Othello. Sapphires eyes lit up. Was he just trying to scare them?

"What's one less nigga on the streets, huh? No one will even miss you when you're gone. It'll be just one less hood boy muddying up our community, living off welfare and government assistance."

The boys were stunned with fear, they looked as if they had seen a ghost.

"Boo!" said Bartholomew and suddenly his gun released one bullet that was so swift, so fast that Sapphire couldn't stop it from penetrating straight into the very heart that belonged to Othello.

"No!" Sapphire screamed as he waved his hand and Bartholomew's gun melted into a pool of black goop.

"What are you?" Bartholomew asked as he backed away, before running off.

Othello took one gust of a breath, fell over and was caught by Sapphire who held his arms under his bloody body. Red blood oozed out of the young magician's chest and ran its way down the gray hoodie he had and drenched the floor.

Tears, lots of them – and sweat slid down Sapphire's face as all he could say was, "no."

Othello was no more.

It felt as if his head had been crumbled to dust, his eyeballs of hot liquid, his heart a prisoner of torture, his muscles burning like fire in his body.

Sapphire looked down at the body of Othello and gazed at his face, but before he could bellow out a cry he thought to himself that there could be a way to fix this.

"You okay," Sapphire said as he brushed the cheek of Othello. "I'm gone fix this...I'm gone get...I'm gone take you to Leonidas he got...he got a s–spell to put things back together. You ain't dead, you ain't dead, just stay with me, Othello, stay...stay. Leonidas is gone heal your heart – he can't take you away from us – you – you're a magician; you've got power flowing through your veins."

Othello wasn't speaking, or moving, but Sapphire still didn't have doubt that he could fix the situation. He closed his eyes and teleported Othello to the second floor of the apartment. When he looked up, as he knelt down with Othello on his arms, he could see that Leonidas and the magicians were all standing around.

Cirrus, Napoleon and Neptune were resting on the

steps behind and Leonidas stood with Calypso on his right, and to his left a woman with a short, black ponytail and a baggy windbreaker; Harmony, his mother.

The woman broke down and screamed for her baby as she placed her hand on Othello's chest.

Calypso touched her back as she looked at Sapphire, she wore a wrinkled, black jumpsuit and her eyeliner had smudged around her glossy cheeks.

"That white...racists...racist police officer shot him, Leonidas," Sapphire spat as he felt his back become hard as a rock, his lungs searing with pain.

"We know," said Calypso, her tears pouring down her face just like everyone else – even Leonidas. "We've been waiting for you two to come back; I foresaw this, all of this."

"Sapphire," Leonidas whispered, "Calypso informed us all about this...an hour ago...."

Everyone seemed to sob more when Othello's mother started to scream. Seeing a mother mourn for her child made her worthy of so much pity. Sapphire imagined what sort of state his mother would be in if her child had been brought home with a bullet in his chest.

Sapphire still knelt down as he held Othello, his stomach being stabbed with the blades of anxiety.

Leonidas dropped to his knees as Calypso placed her arms around his shoulders.

"Our family," Leonidas mumbled, "has just lost yet another brother to a killing by the hands of...of the retched WHITE DEVIL!"

"No, no, no, he's not dead," Sapphire said.his voice shaking, and his eyes twitching, while sweat covered his hands and his face. "Leonidas, you – you have a spell to bring things back together, I would have done it but I couldn't remember the incantation. But you could rejoin his flesh – stop the bleeding."

Something came over Leonidas' face as if he had lost that flavor that was in his personality. Now he just looked lost. No longer fearless, but hopeless.

"Sapphire, listen to me, my brother, please" Leonidas whispered, "I can bring back broken parts and mend cracked objects – even the broken bones of a body, but I cannot bring a soul back to its host once it's been set free by death. Othello...is dead."

17 RETALIATION

Two heavy men, in black, wearing dark shades, carried Othello out with a white sheet over his body. His mother looked sorry, sorry that she couldn't properly say goodbye, sorry that he was gone from this world. She walked down the hall by him as Sapphire still sat, crouched down as he reached out for Othello's body.

He looked up at Leonidas, who stood beside him, his arms around Calypso. "That...that cop just shot him," said Sapphire as he continued to leak tears. "He just shot him for nothing."

Cirrus jumped up and punched at the wall as Neptune ran to her room in a crying fit.

"I know," whispered Leonidas as he could hear the fragile voice of Othello's mother, as the men carried his son down the steps; she followed after them with her hands on her son's bloody sheet. "I know too well," Leonidas scoffed, "of what the white, wicked devils do to our kind. Those retched witch hunters that went after our kind had religious reasons for what they did, at least they believed their cruel killings had a sense of meaning, but these police that are exterminating our black brothers and sisters –"

Leonidas kicked at Napoleon's door hard, his nostrils flared as Calypso tried to grab ahold of him.

"Calm down, brother," she whispered.

"Do not think that we will sit and mourn for long!" Leonidas yelled. "I will not cry in my home, in DISPAIR while I allow his home to have peace. "Napoleon, Cirrus, go get the other leaders, have them get their bodyguards, their guns – whatever they have. Tell 'em that the white devil has taken my brother – our brother out of our hands like a lamb stolen from his heard –"

"Don't kill anyone, Leonidas," Calypso said.

"We won't murder his family like he murdered ours," said Leonidas as Cirrus and Napoleon headed down the steps, "but this officer, Bartholomew; we will install heartache into his community like he has ours. Now, Calypso, you said he's from Carnegie Hill, right?"

"Right," said Calypso as she began to cry more than she had before.

"Well, I need you to look into your crystal ball and get me the names of all the police that patrol near and around that area and write their names down."

"I cannot concentrate –"

"You have to."

"Please, don't make me do this, I –"

"Listen, I know it takes a lot of your concentration," said Leonidas as he walked up to Calypso, causing her to back up into the wall, "but they KILLED him Calypso, and you have to help me get them back – get them all back –

"Let's go burn his house down!" Neptune yelled as she walked out of her room with a bat in her hands."

Sapphire stood up as he tried to remember how to speak after sobbing on the carpet, "I'm with her, I'm ready."

"Calypso, we need you," Leonidas said, his eyes deep into Calypso's. "Please."

"Okay," said Calypso as she slowly walked away to her room. "Okay, fine, and if it kills me, so be it, Leonidas."

She walked into her room as she covered her mouth to quiet her crying.

Leonidas ran up to Sapphire who's brown skin was slick with his tears. He stood still as Leonidas grabbed his shoulders to say, "my dear, Sapphire, brotha', tonight we will destroy his territory, we will be heard, we will go into the quiet and peaceful neighborhood in Carnegie Hill and we will roar so loud that no one will have peace."

"No justice...no peace," Sapphire whispered as Leonidas caressed his cheeks.

"That's right, no justice no peace. But I'm gonna need you to stand with me," a tear slid down Leonidas's face, "stand with me and allow me to channel your wonderful...mighty power so that we can all teleport there and leave without a trace. Those pigs will not put any of us in their cells."

"Okay," said Sapphire, "whatever you say, Leonidas."

And after that, many things took place, all at the same time. Calypso wrote the names of the police that patrolled near Carnegie Hill and handed them to Leonidas who was painting his face into the image of a white skull with black circles around his eyes. Napoleon and Cirrus grabbed their guns, and announced outside to the other gangs that they would shoot any police on sight if they saw them.

A glass cup was placed on top of a table in the room where talent night was held as Leonidas gathered Calypso, Neptune and Sapphire around as the names of the police were placed into it.

"A voodoo sleeping spell, I use it to aid my insomnia…puts me to sleep for eight hours," said Leonidas as he and the others touched hands in the circle. "Everyone close your eyes and allow me to draw from your strength."

Being channeled, to Sapphire, felt like having his blood drawn, but less uncomfortable.

Leonidas looked up, and yelled out his incantation, "Losunga Popajio Regingo Poppaja Jaa," then, the names in the glass burst into flames until there was nothing left in the cup but ash.

Where ever they were, whoever they were, they fell, whether in cars or on patrol; the police were asleep. They caused crashes as they drove into stores and slammed into other cars. A disaster was manifesting.

Leonidas and Sapphire walked outside to be with the rest, who were all putting on black balaclava's and ski mask over their faces. Sapphire was given a black scarf from Napoleon to tie around his face, covering his mouth and hiding his appearance. Cirrus handed him a bat and he took it swiftly.

The people of Boon Hood had become a mob surrounding Leonidas, they all yelled out in disgust, hurt evident on their faces.

Alexandrite stood with her man by her side, both in long black leather jackets as Machiavelli and Crystal revved up their gun strapped motorcycle engines.

"Only the leaders are coming with us," said Leonidas as he scanned the mob, "if anything happens to my people I will blame myself." He looked over at Calypso as she entered into the chaotic crowd, "Calypso, you stay here —"

"Why, because I'm a woman, Neptune's going?" Calypso asked.

Leonidas touched Calypso's face, "I know you wanna come —"

"I am coming —"

"You're not. You're not coming — because if anything happens to me you'll be...you'll be the next ruler of Boon Hood — understand me — you'll be this families queen."

Calypso looked down at her feet and then slowly turned away, but before entering into Osiris she turned back and said, "well, you rattle their cages for me, since I can't go! Don't kill anyone like they have done countless amount of times, but you snatch peace from his children — from his wife — FROM HIS WHOLE COMMUNITY!"

Everyone had burst in agreement as Calypso ran back inside to her room.

"You heard her," Leonidas yelled. "We will not allow his community to be in peace. We will be heard! No justice no peace!"

The people of Boon Hood bellowed with a loud, "Yaaaa!" Leonidas touched Sapphire's arm, channeled his magic and said, "we mourn our fallen brother in black," and suddenly everyone's clothing turned a deep black as dark as a crows eye. Leonidas summoned his father's war staff and slammed its end into the ground.

"Let's go!" Machiavelli roared as he and Crystal circled around Leonidas.

"I'll be back, my sweet," said Alexandrite as she kissed her lover goodbye. She hissed and revealed her fangs, ready for action.

"Everyone, stand around me," Leonidas yelled as he touched Sapphire's arm once again to channel, "we will teleport to our safe house in Queens, once we have finished our destruction, we will leave before those filths can throw us behind their bars!"

Leonidas closed his eyes, and in a puff of black smoke, the magicians, Alexandrite, Machiavelli and Crystal all vanished from view.

In the quiet neighborhood of Carnegie Hill, as the sun burned down, they appeared in a tremendous heap of smoke and took in the view of a block with brownstone townhomes across the street from a park.

They all just stood, waiting for Leonidas to give an order.

The voodoo king spat on the ground, cursed it and pointed to the brownstone townhouses, "this is where the murderer who took our brother lives. This is his humble community. Destroy it all!"

Everyone advanced on the neighborhood and went in for destruction. Crystal and Machiavelli raced off on their motorcycles as they shot at parked cars and into the air so that everyone living in the townhomes would duck down from their windows.

Sapphire charged at a nearby, car and cracked at its exterior, breaking in its windows and screaming while doing so. He kicked at its frame and busted the headlights, but that wasn't enough for him, he set the car on fire and it exploded

Neptune and Napoleon busted up a van, and like Sapphire, who was burning cars by just walking by them, set it on fire.

"Into their homes!" roared Leonidas as he shot beams of green light from his Scepter towards the park across the street, causing its features to burn up in crackling flames.

Alexandrite, Cirrus, and Napoleon kicked in the doors and ran through the homes, causing screams and placing fear into all the residents' hearts, as they ran around trashing everything in sight. Families were pinned to hide in their rooms at gunpoint while money was taken, furniture was destroyed and walls and ceilings were shot at.

A fire truck had headed towards the street and as Sapphire turned to see it approach him he raised his hands and their tires exploded, making their truck turn over.

Three police cars drove up on the other side of Leonidas and got out with guns in their hands. Before any triggers were pulled, Leonidas banged his staff on the street and a burst of gray smoke sprouted up from his staff's end and gusted into their eyes and blinded them all.

On either side were burning cars, melting and coiling up as police officers struggled to walk around without being able to see. They touched at their tender eyes that they could barely open, as they complained about not being able to see anything in sight. Leonidas shot at one of their cars and it exploded as one police officer who yelled in pain announced that it was a bomb. But it was no bomb. The voodoo king had wanted to use his father's war staff for so long and to see its thundering power made his heart swell inside.

He turned to see Sapphire who had the entire fire crew dancing a jig under his mind control spell.

"Sapphire," yelled Leonidas, "his home is the middle one. Go. Burn it down!"

Sapphire ran into the middle townhouse that had

its door knocked off the hinges and entered into a bedroom where a Caucasian woman with two little girls stood.

He looked at their faces, all of them frightened for their lives. He couldn't burn up a home, Leonidas had said that they wouldn't kill anyone. He looked down at the mother of Bartholomew's children, rollers in her blond hair a nightgown covering her body.

"You know how many cops it takes to change a light bulb!?" Sapphire yelled as the mother grabbed a hold of her girls even tighter. "Well, that depends on how long they take to beat the wall for being black!"

Sapphire smashed a hole in the pot belly television set in the room and then scattered around trinkets and treasures on their dresser, including photographs and heirlooms, as the children cried out in fear.

To hear them scream made him feel a yank at his heart.

"We've gotta go! Helicopters are coming!" Leonidas roared as everyone retreated from the townhouses and ran towards him with money in their pockets, goods in backpacks and hands full of jewelry.

Sapphire had run out of Bartholomew's home and ran out into the street to see that a helicopter was hovering towards their area.

Crystal sped up to Sapphire and he teleported onto his motorcycle as he gripped his bat in his hand. Leonidas examined the chaos he and the others had created one last time, and before the helicopter above could get a clear view, and before more police, who had been called in to aid the neighborhood, could advance on them, they all vanished.

The mob appeared in a wide garage that was big enough for a bus. All around them were old trashed artifacts, broken stools, crooked tables and dirty remains of antiques.

Sapphire stood by Leonidas as everyone cheered that they had made it out alive like Leonidas had said they would. Everyone bragged about the damage they had done as Sapphire looked up at Leonidas who noticed his fallen composure.

With tears still in his eyes, Sapphire buried his head in Leonidas's bosom, sniffling as he imagined the horror on the children that belonged to Bartholomew. Leonidas wrapped his arms around his shivering body and squeezed him tight.

Sapphire thought on all the trauma he had been a part of, all the destruction, yet again another fire.

A tall Latino man walked into the garage with a rifle at his hip and tan coveralls on. He had similar features that Leonidas had, but instead of a bushy afro he had a trimmed fade.

"Orion, it's good to see you," said Leonidas as he broke away to embrace Orion.

"Is that…was that you all out there?" Orion asked as he looked at Leonidas.

"We're on the news?" Leonidas asked with wide eyes.

"Well, not really, homes, they think it's Al Qaeda," said Orion as he looked around at everyone that slowly head nodded at him. "They're saying its terrorist attacking, in all black, wearing ski masks and carrying weapons."

"Just like the media to feed the world the first thing that comes off the top of their heads," said Leonidas.

"You know why they think its Al Qaeda, don't you?" Orion asked as he looked at Leonidas.

"I know, because of that bombing at Grand Central, last month," said Leonidas.

"And the bank bombing before dat," Orion said, "you all are off the hook cause they're just saying it's another Muslim attack. They reported that cops were drugged by them but I know that you must've used that sleeping juju you used to use on me, homes when I couldn't sleep after cuzo' died."

"Sho' is," said Leonidas.

"Man, ain't no drug gone put that many cops to sleep yo", only by the power of my cousin, the voodoo king himself!"

Orion and Leonidas slapped hands. "We just need to lie low, for an hour," said Leonidas, "I'll tell you why we trashed Carnegie Hill in your room, it's a little rough, you might wanna sit down."

"Cool," said Orion as he beckoned for every to grab drinks from a freezer in his garage.

"Everyone, we're laying low here, for a while," Leonidas said, "until I'm done talking with Orion in his room."

Sapphire stayed behind and sat on Crystal's parked motorcycle as he tried to stop himself from crying.

What had he just done?

An hour and a half later, he sat in his room with a wet pillow that had been absorbing all his tears. He usually would write when it got dark in his apartment, but all he could do was let out screeching sobs. The news reporters were going on about Al Qaeda and eyewitnesses, who claimed they had seen Muslims in black, patrol near the area. One news channel had gotten word that none of the residents in Carnegie Hill wanted to speak directly to the camera, as they feared for their lives.

Just as a report came in on the sleeping police that was brought into the hospital, Cirrus tapped on Sapphire's door.

Sapphire got up in his blue pajamas and a tank top to answer

Cirrus's looked very tired and drunk, but could say the words, "Leonidas wants you upstairs," just fine.

In the room, where talent night was held, Sapphire and Cirrus walked in to see Leonidas on his knees, in tears, while a wall in front of him carved into the image of a black boy with cornrows: Othello.

Neptune and Napoleon sat in metal chairs as Calypso sat in the back on a burgundy fainting couch with Othello's mother next to her.

When they were trashing Carnegie Hill, the clouds above were a gloomy gray but now they released rain, bullets of it, streaming against the windows.

Leonidas stood up and turned towards Sapphire. "I called you up here to help me do one last thing," said Leonidas as he beckoned for Napoleon to bring over a black cauldron that he played on the floor between Sapphire and Leonidas. "I have promised Harmony that we would get justice for her because if she goes to the ones who murdered her son for justice she will not receive it. A hex, one that is not as painful as being shot in the chest but almost as bitter…I'm going to make that pig feel the same pain he made Othello feel. And I need your help, Sapphire."

"Will he die?" Sapphire asked his eye's twitching.

"No…no…I'm about to perform a ritual, from my ancestors, called the Ontplofo Harro Hex, it only – causes severe heart pain, but he will not die."

"Why…why can't anyone else do it, Leonidas? I'm tired–"

"The ritual requires the blood of a virgin," said Leonidas, "and no one else in Boon Hood is. And, with your magic, it can reach him no matter how far he is."

"I don't know–"

"Come on, Sapphire," Leonidas said as he began to bite his lip, a tear falling down his face, "think about how it felt when he did it. Think about the pain Othello, your brother, my brother, her son felt. Think about how that bullet pierced his skin, killing him instantly! You didn't even get a chance to say goodbye."

Harmony collapsed over on Calypso who began to cry herself.

Everyone else watched Leonidas and Sapphire, wondering what would happen next. "Fine…I'll do it," Sapphire said as he looked at Leonidas in his compelling eyes. He didn't need to use his mind control spell on Sapphire because his tears had persuaded him to do so.

"The ritual will overtake us and cause us to perform the sacred dance in sync. One pure, and one defiled, one virgin and one no longer."

Leonidas was given a knife from Neptune and he

took ahold of Sapphire's hand to slit his palm.

"Ahhh," Sapphire said as he felt a surge of pain go up his arm before Leonidas had healed him of his cut. The blood from Sapphire's hand dripped from Leonidas's knife and splattered into the cauldron.

Leonidas lit a match and threw it in after, causing a burst of red flames to gust upwards as he said the words, "Ontplofo Harro." He looked around and said, "we need music, the ritual needs to be edified, everyone clap after me."

Leonidas clapped his hands above his head and everyone repeated his rhythm.

Sapphire looked down at the smoke from the cauldron.

"Inhale the smoke, Sapphire, let it in," Leonidas said as he himself allowed the smoke into his nostrils.

Together, with no hesitation, the two began to dance. They moved as if they wanted to perfectly copy one another's moves, Leonidas would raise his hand up and Sapphire would do it at the same time. The two leaped around and waved their hands around. The flames of the cauldron grew as the two magicians danced around it, their eyes on one another, their bodies moving in ways that Africans had danced in culture films and on documentaries that Sapphire had seen. The rituals power made him move in these ways, he wanted to, or at least it made him want to.

Leonidas, with his curly afro bopping around and his swinging arms waving, dipped down and twirled around while Sapphire did the exact same thing, becoming one in their minds.

As they went on, Bartholomew shivered and shook around in his sleep as he rested in his hospital bed. A nurse came into his room to see him jerking around while his eyes remained closed. Sapphire and Leonidas turned towards the fire, spat in into it, then the cauldron cracked in half and the heart of Bartholomew exploded.

18 HOME

It was 7:00 am in the morning, Sapphire, under his thick blanket, sat up as he looked at his television. Last night was a sleepless night. He had cried so much that he didn't think he could release any more tears. He looked at his television and it watched him more than he did it until he heard a news report that announced that everyone's dear neighborhood police officer, Bartholomew Wallace, had died from a heart rupture, the night before.

The blanket was slid back, the bed's weight had been lifted and Sapphire stood in a shaking tremble as he looked at the news report. Streams of tears slid their way down to his mouth and he could taste their salty flavor. He opened his mouth but only a whisper of a frail squawk came out. He was choking on guilt. The dreadhead convinced himself that he was now a murderer.

Bartholomew's children would never see their father again and his wife would have to raise them alone. The horror of killing a man rose up Sapphire's throat and sprouted out his mouth into a loud scream.

Leonidas couldn't properly answer his door because it had flown off its hinges as he sat up in his bed

Sapphire walked in with red eyes and a heap of sweat covering his face, "you lied to me!"

Leonidas jumped up. "What?"

"The hex, you lied to me – Bartholomew is dead!" Sapphire said. "Did you not think I would watch the news, Leonidas? He died of a heart rupture last night at the very same time we performed the –"

"What other choice did I have!?" Leonidas asked as he slammed his hand on his dresser. "What other choice…when Harmony came over, and we broke the news to her, I told her that I would get revenge for her – I – would murder this pig! He deserved it, that was our brother – our friend and he got shot for doing nothing, Sapphire!"

"Well, what about his kids, man?" Sapphire asked as he balled up his fist. "They don't have a father now, we lost a brother and now they don't have a father –"

"Sounds like a fair deal to me," spat Leonidas. His eyes were cold, his lips pressed together.

Sapphire backed away as the hurt of taking another life settled deeper into his young heart. "You're a murderer; you're a murderer just like your father."

"Shut up!" Leonidas roared. "Don't talk about my father – those police pigs deserve to be tortured, endlessly, for killing his best friend, but he gave them mercy by giving them death. How long can we sit back while they kill us off, how long will it be before they shoot you next? Calypso saw it all in her vision they had no right to search you all and press your faces up against the wall –"

"So, you forced me to kill him with you?" Sapphire asked. "And when…and when I asked you if this – voodoo ritual – would kill him you lied to me just to fulfill your bloodlust…."

Leonidas didn't speak, and Sapphire backed away
even further as he saw the same carelessness that was
in Seraphina's eyes and in the man that she betrayed
him with. Once again another deception, another
trick instead of a treat; someone else had taken their
toll on his soul and did not care.

"I'm leaving," he whispered as he left out of
Leonidas' room.

"Sapphire – no," Leonidas said as he watched
Sapphire run out and head for his apartment on the
second floor. Leonidas kicked at his dresser and sat
on his bed with his face buried in his hands, as
Sapphire swiftly changed into a sweater and jeans. He
left his remaining clothes but picked up his grimoire
and backpack. As he placed his black fedora over his
head he looked at himself in his bathroom mirror and
tried not to cry as he rubbed at his drowsy eyes.

Leonidas walked in just as he grabbed his black
leather jacket.

"Please, don't go," he said as he looked at
Sapphire, who stood still, not taking his searing eyes
off him. "Please, I can't lose two of my brothers in
one week, don't go –"

"Move, Leonidas," Sapphire said as he rolled his
eyes.

With his hands together, Leonidas walked closer
to Sapphire and looked at him with sincerity in his
eyes, but Sapphire shoved around him and walked out
of his apartment room.

"Sapphire!" Leonidas said as his voice compelled
Sapphire to stop in his tracks and turn around.

"What, Leonidas?" Sapphire asked. "What?"

"What was I supposed to do…let that foul
murderer go free, and get a paid vacation like that

other cop that killed that black kid?

"Leonidas, I –"

"Tell me how should a man act when the boy he helped raised, nurtured when his own mother abandoned him – watched him grow up for three years – how was I supposed to react?"

Leonidas reached out his hand for Sapphire as everyone came out of their rooms. Napoleon, Cirrus, Neptune and Calypso stood outside of their doors as Leonidas begged for Sapphire to stay.

"Sapphire, don't go now!" Neptune said as she rested her head on her door frame.

"Yeah, boy, you can't leave us too," said Cirrus.

"Well, I am," said Sapphire as he turned around to examine everyone that was watching him with sorrowful eyes. "I love all of you, and you've been a wonderful family to me, but I cannot stay here anymore – do you all know what he did to me!?"

"Sapphire, please just wait," said Calypso as she looked as if she had been crying even more.

"Don't go, man, we can't keep losing everyone," Napoleon said as Neptune began to cry in her hands.

"Here," said Sapphire as he tossed his grimoire at Leonidas, "keep the grimoire so that everyone can continue to learn. I've studied its pages…and you all need it more. Hopefully, it will pay my debt for living here for free. I left my room key on the TV, now, I'm out of here. Goodbye."

Sapphire turned to walk and no one stopped him, but as he approached the steps, he noticed that his legs couldn't move. Behind him, with his right arm stretched out, stood Leonidas as he held onto the grimoire. "Don't go…brother, I love you."

"Let me go," said Sapphire.

"Leonidas, don't," said Calypso.

"Ever since you came into my home I knew you were...I knew you were special even before I knew you were a superior –"

A tear fell down Sapphire's face, "Let me go, Leonidas."

"And I wanted to protect you and show you that you could have a home after being hurt by so many others...I never meant to hurt you either, I thought you'd understand – you didn't kill anyone it was all me. I tricked you into doing it, you had no idea – don't blame yourself."

"Leonidas."

"I just need you to please –"

"Let go!" Sapphire yelled as Leonidas's body was thrown towards the back steps that led to the third floor.

The voodoo king, in front of his people, was embarrassed by Sapphire as he overpowered him with his superior might. Without any other words, Sapphire excited from Osiris, away from 207, away from his new family and away from the ghost of Othello, who he believed resided in the halls and rooms where they enjoyed each other's company.

He didn't want to have breakfast in the kitchen anymore; he didn't want to play games in Cirrus's room anymore, not without his friend.

As he stepped out in the chilly weather of the morning he could see Crystal leaning against an El Camino, with his brother Topaz and a young girl with hardly any clothes on.

"Hey, Sapphire," said Crystal as he waved.

Sapphire hesitated. "Hey, Crystal."

He proceeded to walk down and headed out with

intentions to never return to Boon Hood ever again.

He waved at everyone that he knew as they traded drugs on the street, drank and smoke. Some asked where he was going and he responded that he was going to the store, but he was really on his way back home. He needed his mother now, more than ever.

Too much had happened and nothing else could save him from his despair but his mother's love that soothed his soul. He realized as he walked on, that the reason he could not hurt Cerberus and Seraphina or take any of Bartholomew's family was because he had his mother's same love in his heart. The compassion that his mother had passed down to him through birth was nurtured in his heart as she raised him, and he was grateful for that.

As he turned a left corner and headed towards a bus seat, he saw a little kid, a black girl with long pigtails was playing hopscotch by herself, and after she finished she spun into a Fouette. That reminded him of Othello and how well he could spin. Sapphire walked up to her and told her that she was beautiful and that her future was bright. It was as if everything he hadn't got to say to Othello came out to her and that made him feel a spark in his heart. The fire was not gone yet, the chance to smile again was still there, somewhere under all the grief.

He knelt down to her, "I knew a guy that could spin just like that," he paused as the little girl looked down at him, her braces revealed when she smiled. "I couldn't tell him all the things I wanted to – or should have because he...he's gone. But, but I want you to know that you are beautiful, and you can be anything you want to be. And you keep on spinning and winning and be a Ballerina or an engineer or whatever you want to be (his eyes became glossy) because you're our future. You're a strong, beautiful black girl – if no one else ever tells you."

"Thank you," said the little girl as Sapphire backed away from her.

This felt great, this felt worthy of getting up out of bed every morning. If he could continue to encourage children, in which he considered the purest thing on earth then maybe that would drive out the guilt he held in his heart.

"You're beautiful," he said as he remembered how Othello confessed that he didn't think he was attractive. "You're beautiful."

Sapphire continued on down the street and saw two more children walking down with their mother. "You're beautiful," he said as he ran up to them, startling their mother. Tears began to run down his face as he kept on moving, then he stopped as he saw a little girl getting her hair braided outside of an apartment building.

"You are beautiful, you are beautiful," he chanted as he began to sob even more.

Was he having a nervous breakdown, or was he being released from his depression? Even his own father, who was hard like stone, would say that tears let out the hearts issues and was necessary, so he cried out while adorning this neighborhood with compliments.

He had passed his bus stop accidentally and kept on until he walked past a man with dark skin, gray hair and a black and red pinstriped suit.

"My brother, do you know Jesus as your personal Lord and savior?" he asked as he stood under a neon sign that read: Joy of The Word, non-denominational.

"What?" Sapphire said as he turned to look at the man who stood with his hands folded.

"Do you know Jesus?" he asked again.

"I don't know...is that your idea of God?" Sapphire asked.

"What is your name, boy?" the man asked.

"I'm Sapphire Bell."

"Well, Sapphire, I'm Pastor Ruby."

"Listen, Pastor, I ain't had such a good start off on my day and all this Jesus talk ain't gone make it no better, it's just confusing and it makes my head hurt. Thank you, though."

And after that Sapphire walked away, but before he could leave Pastor Ruby said, "alright now, son, but the wages of sin is death. Whenever you ready to turn from your life of pain and turn it over to God we'll be right here, Saturday, Sunday, Monday, and Wednesday."

Sapphire heard him clearly, but did not respond, and did not think he needed to.

He caught a bus, headed towards home and was dropped off a block behind his mother and father's Townhouse. As he approached the street, the words of Pastor Ruby had sat on his heart. How he knew of his life of pain was a mystery, but he tried to shake that thought off as his footsteps touched the porch of his parents' home. In an instant, his mother answered. In a caramel sweater and brown slacks was Marquette, and she looked happier than ever as she answered her door.

She hugged him and squeezed him tight. She made cocoa, sat him down in the living room and made him tell her all about his stay at a shelter for magicians, while they faced each other in brown leather chairs. He explained everything about Boon Hood but left out all the bad details to satisfy his mother's mind, but he didn't spare the details on his break up with Seraphina. She thought it was a bad joke, his mother did, that both of them had been hurt and cheated on and disrespected by the ones they loved so dearly.

Sapphire smiled as his mother tried to slide in a joke to make him laugh while he expressed his sadness. She always would do that – she would slip a joke in to melt Sapphire's heart when it was icy cold. She knew the spell, she had the magic to take his soul and rejuvenate it.

A mother's love was a powerful force, according to Sapphire.

After laughing at a few of his stories with his mother he asked a question, "how is dad?"

Marquette rolled her eyes as she began to think back on her soon to be ex-husband.

He pulled out a poem from his backpack that he had written for his mother, and before he read it, he looked up at her to say, "I know you don't really wanna talk about daddy, but where is he? I don't wanna stay here if he's coming back."

"He's not," said Marquette as her long fingernails slid back her bang. "He's got all his stuff out and he's staying at a hotel. I probably won't stay here for long, either, I might get me a little job and get us an apartment...cause I don't wanna live off him at all."

"Me neither," said Sapphire as he unwrinkled his poem. "Mama, I... wanted to read you a poem since you and me ain't really got to talk about this whole divorce thing."

"You so sweet, baby," said Marquette as she

226

leaned up from her seat, crossing her legs. "Let me hear it, please."

"Okay," said Sapphire as his eyes lit up, "I hope you like it."

And he read:

"Dearest mother, your chains are cracked, your back is straightened; your days of being daddy's handmaid have come to an end. And now your name has changed, but, don't think I have forgotten you. I remember you just as well.

You were a caged dove and now you've been set free, spread your beautiful, white wings and fly, but don't fly too close to the sun, mother of angels, less your wings burn. My dear, you were his secretary but now you are your own boss. You were his destiny, my beautiful queen, but he couldn't finish it with you. You were his love letter that he barely opened, and now you've rewritten it.

"Because both of you were born in the fall, every time I see the leaves change I'll remember how your love seemed to do the same. Like your relationship, the leaves of love's tree came tumbling to the ground in crusty piles. Crunchy under my feet. But the fall leaves change colors and rain over me in unison, unlike you two, they know how much I'll miss seeing you both together.

"He called you moon and you called him sun, but now I've noticed a new galaxy has begun. Mama, don't ever think I won't remember who you were and who you are. You were my everything. Precious soul, gentle soul, brave heart, lion heart, I remember you."

"Oh, my goodness, that's so good, Sapphire," she said as she got up to hold him in her arms and that made him smile.

227

He hadn't told her of all the things that were on his mind like Othello's death or being tricked into performing a voodoo murder ritual, but somehow she received all of his hurt through her arms being wrapped around him.

They stayed that way for about a minute, and after a few hours of talking and eating sandwiches together, Sapphire walked into his room that his mother had cleaned.

As the sun began to set through his window it beamed against his eyes, so he closed his auburn curtains. He looked around and examined the things he had left behind. Paintings he hadn't finished, books he hadn't completely dived into, and some of his favorite clothes that he didn't have enough room for when he was packing his things.

When he remembered how he had left he thought about his father being slammed up against the wall by his own magic. He didn't know if he'd ever say sorry to him because he didn't know if he'd ever call him again.

19 GHOST

After a much-needed shower, he changed into a cream sweater and black pajama pants. Sapphire had sniffled a little after a breakdown in his shower. He was hurting bad, he was being haunted.

Something — someone wouldn't let his spirit rest. The ghost of Othello crept around his mind and lounged in his memory bank. He couldn't see a transparent image of a ghost but could hear his voice and even smell his clothes that were always soaked with cologne stolen from Cirrus. He could feel Othello, in his heart and in his mind.

Ghost stories were never scary to Sapphire nor were ghost movies; however, the ghost of his past was terrifying.

Out of all his ghost, he couldn't decide which one was more scarier. Was it the ghost of blood, the blood that splashed from Othello's chest? Was it the dead look on his face? That ghost haunted him as well. Maybe it was the ghost of murder, its red grimacing face creeping in Sapphire's memories, screaming in a most intolerable voice, "you murdered! You murdered!"

Was it the ghost of guilt? Was it the green ghost of self-hate that crept like a demon up his wall, looking at him dead in his eyes as if it wanted to eat his soul? Was it the ghost of failure's past? Was it the

229

ghost of depressions present? Was it the ghost of the dreaded future that he might not ever see peace or even rest again, without waking in a screaming fit?

Othello had died a horrible and nasty death, Sapphire never even got to lie to him with a promise that he would be okay, or that he would heal from his piercing gunshot. He died before he even hit the ground.

And he held him. He kept him in his arms; no one else was there but him. And now, as he entered his room, an idea came into mind. He couldn't bring a soul back to its body, but, perhaps he could communicate with the soul. He stretched out his hands and lifted them up high. There wasn't any spell that he had heard of for speaking with the dead but he was ready to try it out – even without an incantation (which made all spell casting easier).

He was ready to tell him all the things he'd never gotten the chance to say. He wanted one last time to give him some confidence, give him some assurance that he mattered in this world.

Didn't he deserve that. Didn't every young man and woman deserve to know that they were important and that even in the event that their own birth parents neglected them that someone out there should tell them? Sapphire was raised to believe he was something. His mother made him chant with a shout, "I'm black and I'm proud!" He was raised to know that he didn't deserve someone who didn't value him, or care, even if that person was beautiful like Seraphina.

He had to make contact with Othello's ghost. Nothing was going stop him.

He concentrated hard on Othello, as he tried to summon the spirit of his fallen friend. He could see that the lights in his room were shining bright green, blue, then red. Things were beginning to float and he was brought to his knees as he felt a shock to his spine. His magic wasn't able to perform this action. He rested on his knees in a crying fit as he gripped a hold of his hands.

As the lights in his room continued to change their color he knew that it was because of his magic being spun out of control by his lack of knowledge. He had great power but much to learn about how to wield it.

Things rattled and buzzed. A photograph of him as a boy flew across the room. The walls were illuminated by whatever odd colors were burning from anything that gave off light and even his dresser and closet doors seemed to have a life of their own as the superior spell caster tried his hardest to use unlearned skills of spiritual communication.

He cried as hard as his throat would allow as he found out that there were forces that even superior spell casters couldn't control.

His head rolled, neck popped and he yelled, "I just wanna speak to him!"

Tears fell. Tears soaked his lap.

"Please!" he cried out. "Please. Please."

Who was he pleading with? He didn't know. Maybe God was listening, he thought. And if God was listening he could answer his cry? Just one chance to talk to him. One sweet goodbye.

"I wanna speak to him! I just wanna speak to him! Othello! I'm so sorry!"

He collapsed, feeling weak and humbled by the fact that he was nothing less than powerless here.

He thought of ghost as images that were able to create sound in the mind and cause the nostril to smell things that were not there. Ghost could touch with no fingers, phase through a body like an invisible train. Ghost could haunt you without getting tired, or without ever caring how bad they made you feel.

Why did he volunteer to take him out, he questioned. If he would have never taken him out none of this would have ever happened.

Before tonight, he would watch films where characters would ask the question, "do you believe in ghosts?"

After hearing this, within himself, he would always say, "no." But now he did. Because ghosts were all over his room, crawling up walls and lurking under bed. They were screaming insults like angry accusers in his head.

But sadly, the only one he wanted as company couldn't respond to his cry. Othello couldn't talk back

Jay Hunter

· 20 GLOOM

While in bed, the night before Wednesday, he looked up at his popcorn ceiling in his room as an orchestra played a dramatic piece on his television. Memories, sweet memories, bad memories, all coursed their way through his young, troubled mind as he stretched his arms out in a T. No one could count his tears; no one could tell how many times he tried to silence his crying as he would place a pillow over his mouth. 1996, to him, was a year he didn't expect to be as brutal as it was.

Sleep wasn't his friend, but depression was trying to be his new lover.

Now, it was Wednesday, in the morning; and after four days of moping around and watching old documentary films on famous artist, Sapphire finally got out of bed and finished a poem that he had started the day before. He was writing comfortably until he heard a song played on his radio.

When I'm With You had come on, and it was as if the song had become more of a haunting rhythm than a sweet love ballad. This song reminded him of his anger towards the woman that tore his heart out. But he also felt for his mother, when hearing it, because this wasn't just their song but three years before, his parents had made it as their song, after renewing their vowels in October.

He finished his poem, and before he could get up to change out of his pajamas he heard his mother call him. He got up and walked downstairs to the hall where his mother stood with a woman in a long, black dress with a burgundy shawl and black boots. Her hair was down both sides of her face and her lips and eyelids were painted bright green.

"Hey," said Sapphire as he stood.

"This lady, Sapphire, she says she knows you and wants to know if she can talk to you about your friend that died – that you didn't tell me about," said Marquette as she looked up at Sapphire.

"Sorry, mom," he said as he walked closer to them. "I'm sorry, I just didn't wanna put so much on you."

Calypso looked very tired, but very eager to speak with him. "If I can, ma'am, just talk to him about the funeral today?"

"It's today?" said Sapphire as he looked at Calypso. "The funeral?"

"Yeah, it's today," whispered Calypso, her eyes glossy.

Of course she had found him by her psychic powers and crystal ball, but did she know inside that he didn't want to go?

"Um, y'all can talk in the living room," said Marquette. "Do you like coffee, Calypso?"

"Um, yes, ma'am," said Calypso as Sapphire led her to the two chairs in the living room. The television was on the news and they were reporting about the policeman that had been blinded before, stating that they still had not received their sight and that made Sapphire swallow hard.

He turned off the television as he got comfortable

in his chair.

"It's...it's been so terrible...back home without you, Sapphire, without the both of you," said Calypso as she threw her shawl around her. "I miss you so much."

"And I miss you all too," said Sapphire as he gripped his hands. "Really...I know you –"

"That you left? No. I'm not upset."

Sapphire chuckled as Calypso finished his sentence.

"Sorry," said Calypso, "being a psychic is just so...annoying at times. I get these random visions and facts in my head, whenever they wanna come, and it's just like ugh, you know. I get really bothered by it."

"Especially when you see visions of death," said Sapphire.

Calypso closed her eyes, "mmhmm, mmhmm, precisely. Yeah, yeah I...I knew two days before that he would die, and then, and then I tried to convince myself that I could, maybe, fix it. I really did, but I predicted...I remembered that I had predicted Cirrus spraining his ankle and he did – I would predict when someone would fall and no matter how I tried to help, they still would. You know what that means?"

Sapphire frowned. "Yeah."

"That means, that when I see....Whatever I see will happen, it will, it will come true." Calypso became teary-eyed as she slid back one of her lengthy braids, "and I gotta put up with that, all day, all my life. You know, I came to talk to you about the funeral and –"

"I'm not going," said Sapphire.

"I just–"

"I said I'm not going," said Sapphire.

Calypso paused. "What?"

"I'm not seeing Leonidas," said Sapphire, "I know he put you up to this."

"No," Calypso said as she handed Sapphire an obituary with Othello's face on the front cover, "I wanted to come and tell you where it was gonna be and ask you to perform one of your poems, I think it would be –"

"Calypso," said Sapphire. "If Leonidas is going to be there then I don't wanna go, I don't want to be within 300 feet of him. I wouldn't touch him with a ten and a half foot pole."

Calypso looked up as Marquette came in with a cup of coffee and handed it to her. "Thanks so much," she said as Marquette stood over by the wall.

"Mama, Calypso was the reason why I came to the shelter," Sapphire said. "She could see that I was in need of an escape…from everything. She helps run it, that's where I met my friend, and…and she's really sweet."

"Wonderful," said Marquette as she heard the phone ring in the kitchen. "Oh, that's probably your Mema calling, she's been calling me every day to make sure I am sure about this divorce."

Marquette walked off to answer the phone as Calypso took a sip of her coffee. "So, you don't want to see Leonidas?"

"At all," said Sapphire. "I'm sure you know why."

"That was your friend, Sapphire, why would you miss your last chance to see his body –"

"Because I see his bloody body in my dreams every night – after I cry myself to sleep. I don't need to…I don't wanna see him dead anymore…I hate it. I hate it all, and I hate Leonidas and if he comes up to me I might hurt him. You might see a sorcerer brawl as big as the ones in the 1800's."

Calypso took another sip, "I think you might wanna rethink that. This might be the last time you see him...."

Sapphire became silent as he watched a tear flow down Calypso's face. "What are you saying?"

"I'm saying that just last night while trying to get over one death I got another vision, but this one was more intense. I fell out into a trance-like dream. This vision was longer, more real. Calypso closed her eyes as she pressed her hands together.

"What did you see?" Sapphire asked.

"I saw my brother fall in love with a woman... she....I will never speak her name, but she's gonna meet him, next year, at our Brethren Gathering, and Crystal's hosting, and it'll be great, but, Leonidas is going to see her, I think she might be one of Machiavelli's cousin's, but, she's going to be perfect for him, everything he ever wanted in a woman. They're gonna have so much in common, so much love...so much charisma, but then, there is gonna come a time where she's gonna do something he doesn't like. He's...he's going to get really mad and he's going to argue with her – and I mean argue – and that's just like my brother to argue someone down when he doesn't like their actions. They're gonna fight on the back of our old firescape, behind the apartment and...he's gonna grab her, she's gonna fight him, you know how girls are, they try to go toe to toe with men."

Calypso began to sob as she put her hands over her face. Sapphire wiped his eye as he took in her words. What was she about to say next?

"She's gonna push him so hard that he's gonna fall off and die from a head injury," Calypso moaned. "And it's gonna tear her apart like its tearing me apart right now and she's gonna become the new Queen of Boon Hood, because he will already have made her his queen and I'll be long gone before then."

Sapphire tried to fight back tears as he could see how much Calypso was hurting. "Why?"

"I can't see him die twice," said Calypso. "It's already hard to see him this down after you two boys left him, he ain't looked this bad since his mother died. But, I'll get at least a year with him and I won't tell 'em about it cause telling a person how they die is more tragic than death itself, they have to live with knowing that. But, but, Sapphire, don't mourn over the inevitable things, mourn over the things that we could've changed and didn't."

"Like me going to the funeral," said Sapphire as he crossed his legs.

"Right," said Calypso. "I know you probably wanna snap Leonidas's head off, but my brother is a sweet man, really – and I'm not neglecting the fact that he's a murderer, I know he is but he ain't just out here killing innocent people –"

Sapphire looked down.

"And it's sad, not only is he smoking now, but he's drinking – he got real drunk last night. He – I had to stop him because he went out driving…and took his war staff with him. He was just blindly shooting at everything. He's so hurt, I know that's not him, but he's so hurt and I had Cirrus take me to go get him on his bike. I stood on the street with my hands up…and I just looked at him, and he drove at me like he wasn't gonna stop, you know, I almost lost my cool, because, I knew that if he'd see me he'd stop driving but he kept going.

"I thought he was going to hit me, I raised my hands and I just kept thinking he wouldn't do it, he wouldn't – but the car never stopped. Cirrus told me to get out of the way but I had to stop him, he could have killed somebody. I stopped the car myself...and that hurt because I used my own strength to save my life – and I wanted him to do that. I wanted him to be a hero, and not put his self-first this time like he did with you...but he disappointed me again. I knew he lied to you, and I'm sorry, I knew he was going to do it."

"But what you see can't be changed, so you figured why try," said Sapphire. "Why try and stop him."

"I watched you take part in it...I sat there and did nothing because part of me wanted him to die, too. It's wrong, I know, but if you could just understand that me and Leonidas aren't the worst people out here. He might've killed but he didn't kill an innocent man. He killed a clan's member. Yes, that cop was a part of the clan. Nothing can be hidden from my crystal ball if I look hard enough into it."

"But he lied to me. His personal bodyguard, his consultant. I put my trust in him."

"Right, but he's going to die one day, which I'm sure will make you happy, but right now just put yourself aside."

"Calypso, I...I don't want him to die."

"You're right, sorry, right. I apologize, Sapphire. I'm just so worked up, I didn't sleep, really I just kept thinking of the little boy I knew growing up. A Mama's boy living in his father's shadow. You know his eyes lit up so bright when he found out that you were a superior spell caster?

"He never thought he was as good as his father because, he didn't inherit his superior power, but…but you know, as I started thinking about him I remembered me when I was a girl. And that really kept me up. I used to think I was so lucky to be able to predict what movies were coming out, what the weather would be like, the dishes my mother made, but when I saw a vision of my mother…abandoning me, actually running away from me when I woke up in that same apartment I live in now…to go back to her life of prostitution, I no longer felt so lucky."

Calypso wiped her eyes yet again as Sapphire leaned into his seat.

"I'll go," he said. "I'll go, but I really just can't be around Leonidas, and I'm not staying for the whole thing. I'll read my poem, I'll stay until then. After that I'm out, I don't need him trying to sidebar with me. I'm so sorry that you're gonna' lose him, but that doesn't change the way I feel about him."

"Well, it's at two, at the…the Scoggins funeral home…not too far – (Sapphire nodded his head) you know where that is?"

"Yeah," said Sapphire, "I know…I'll be there."

"Sapphire was hugged by Calypso and after she let go, she waved goodbye to Marquette who was still on the phone. Sapphire showed her out and thanked her for coming by.

He turned to his mother who could see the heaviness that was on his shoulders.

He dressed in a white collar shirt with a black vest and slacks that swept at his brown dress shoes. After slipping his poem in his pocket, he put his dreadlocks into a ponytail and looked over at the black fedora that Leonidas had given him.

He really loved the hat.

It's black, wide brim, top and suede texture. He put it on over his dreadlocks and looked over at his clock. It was 1:58 pm.

He thought of how he would arrive at the funeral and didn't want to have to walk to a bus stop in his nice clothes. He remembered something – someone who had the perfect style of transportation for a funeral. He closed his eyes and, in a flash, vanished.

In a puff of black smoke, Sapphire was back in the alleyway where he and Othello had last talked together. He looked down at the very spot that they had teleported to and tried to see if he could see any blood. But Instead of blood, he found a game token that must have fallen out of Othello's pocket when he collapsed. Sapphire held the coin close to his heart and then slid it in his pocket.

Being amongst everyone around 5th avenue made him nervous as he held his head down to hide under the brim of his black hat. Bartholomew's wife had refused to publicly speak, due to the fear of her and her children's lives being endangered, but would she ever have the courage to say that she had seen a black boy with dreadlocks cause trauma in her home? She had heard his voice and even looked into his chocolate brown eyes. He feared that her own children would see him in their nightmares and that gave him ones of his own.

It didn't take him long to get to the hotel, in which the same driver that they had seen before, pulled up in his black limousine. Before he could open his car door he gazed at Sapphire who stood directly in front.

"All he wanted was to ride," Sapphire whispered, "just one...ride, and you wouldn't give it to him." He spoke the incantation, "Zomb Zing Zo."

The driver immediately lost color in his eyes that were now a milky white as his mouth opened wide. Sapphire walked to the side of the limousine, opened the back door and got inside. As he felt the black leather on the seats he commanded the driver to head to Scoggins funeral home.

Without delay, the driver took off, leaving behind a very frustrated old woman who stormed out a half minute later. He wasn't asking, he was making the calls now, and as he sat back he imagined how much fun it would be to ride around with Othello.

He slid out the obituary and sat it right next to him. He pointed out noteworthy buildings and talked to the program as if it was the real thing. He didn't question his sanity because he was having too much fun laughing at all the many jokes they had shared together, all the games they had played, all the times they had made Cirrus upset.

He was in Boon Hood a short time with Othello, but it was long enough to establish a brotherly bond worth crying over.

"Stop, right here is fine," said Sapphire as he approached the red-bricked funeral home. If you have to go use the restroom, go to a gas station, but be back immediately. Understand?" The driver gave a childish nod as Sapphire smoothed out his vest, "oh, and come get my door, man."

The driver got out of his car and opened Sapphire's door, while letting out an, "aaarrgghhh."

"Now go back inside, before someone thinks you're a creep'," said Sapphire as he patted the driver's chest.

The clouds were still gray out, but a burning shard of light had cut through them as Sapphire walked up the steps that led to the front door. He was fifteen minutes late but was sure that he wasn't next up on program yet. With a big gulp, and a deep breath, he walked into the funeral home that had two long rows of pews and almost all of them were filled with family members, what he guessed were school staff and all of Boon Hoods people.

He noticed Crystal and Topaz, who were next to Machiavelli and Alexandrite. He waved at a drunk Nicoleto and winked at Calypso who sat by Cirrus, Napoleon, Neptune and the voodoo king, Leonidas, who wore a black suit with a white tie. Sapphire had never seen him in a suit before and although he hated to see him he couldn't deny within himself that he looked very clean today.

"Come sit with us," whispered Neptune, while a tall, black man in a jogging suit gave a speech on his great nephew.

"No, I'm fine," said Sapphire as he looked upward and made eye contact with Leonidas. He felt a strike of lightning in his heart as he quickly looked away and sat upward by a heavy set woman in a Dalmatian coat, she was sobbing so much that she didn't notice him sit beside her.

He looked forward to an auburn casket that held his friend and looked down at his feet as tears didn't ask permission before sliding down his face.

After Othello's great uncle had spoken, Crystal went up next. After Crystal, Cirrus got up and talked about all the times Othello would steal his stuff and lie about the food he would take from Neptune's room.

"He would want us all to laugh right now," said Cirrus as he rested his hands on the wooden podium. "He wouldn't let me ever cry when I would come home, after failing to mend my relationship with my brother. He would always make me laugh and be that little brother that everybody needed to get...through. I know we all hurt when we think of how he died, but at least we know that that officer that took his life is gone too. And it's crazy that his funeral is today, and it's probably even crazier that they had died on the same day but that's...but anyway I got off topic. I just wanna say that I'll miss you, Othello. We love you."

No one else from Osiris wanted to speak so Leonidas stood up and stepped up to the wooden podium.

"I knew Othello, because I found him after he got kicked out his mom's, and I took him in and he lived in my apartment building for three years with me. I wouldn't charge him anything cause...cause I love my black brotha's and we already have to pay for being black every day anyway."

Sapphire chuckled as he looked up at Leonidas. He didn't look as happy as usual, but he was still the same Leonidas as before.

"I loved him," said Leonidas, "and was deeply hurt when I found out a policeman had shot him. Because I love his whole family as well, I covered everything, hoping that you all would accept me for not protecting him as best as I could. I wanted to say a lot to Othello, and I didn't, so I'm making sure that I say everything that I need to say to a person here before they go. Like how sorry I am for getting caught up in my own selfish ways," he made eye contact with Sapphire as he became careful of his words. "I...I am so sorry to anyone here who I've hurt and can't win back into my life."

Leonidas wiped at his face. Sapphire sat back as he gripped his poem in his hand.

"I wish that everyone learns here today that you've got to get out every selfish piece of your body so you can focus on other's feelings. Because you could look up one day and that person's gone for good."

Calypso began to cry as Leonidas took his seat. The funeral conductors asked if there was anyone else that wanted to give remarks and after no one else got up they asked for a poem to be read by Sapphire Silas Bell.

As he got up and walked through the aisle of piercing eyes he walked up to Othello who rested inside his casket. He took out his token and slid it in the pocket of his blue suit jacket that he had been placed in. "You know," he whispered as everyone watched him from behind, "my daddy used to tell me, when I was a kid, that there's a place that young people go after they die called dream station. And...and a train takes them away to a paradise in the galaxy, where there's endless games, food and...good fun. Take this token, and use it to beat everybody, until I get there with some more."

Sapphire turned around and looked at everyone who waited for him to read his poem. He saw

Harmony, Othello's mother, sitting on the front row in black as a young, spiky-haired man hung his arm around her. This had to be his mother's boyfriend, the man that Othello didn't like very much. He was the reason he got into arguments with his mother. Sapphire wondered why he hadn't come to Boon Hood to be with his mother as Othello's body was driven away. Did he really care about Othello or was he just here because he wanted to satisfy his girlfriend's wishes?

"Some of you all don't know me, but I was a friend of Othello's and...I lived in the apartment with him. I was there when he had got...I'm gone be brief." Sapphire placed his poem on the podium and shortened the microphone stand a little lower. "It's called...."

He paused as he wiped his eyes and looked up to the ceiling for a reason not to just leave now and save everyone from him screaming out in pain. Focus, he thought. Just focus.

"The poem is called On a Subway Ride Home," he licked his lips, "and I hope you all find some meaning to it.

And he read:

"Last night...I finally could get sleep. With feet swelled from pacing, head throbbing and chest pains, I crossed my fingers in hopes of no nightmares this time. I sipped my water and convinced myself that sleep was the answer to my depression. I felt the sheets smooth against my tired body, my cover over my legs, they hurt so bad, I know I must've walked two hours; just thinking while doing so.

"In a dream, I was on a subway train – headed where – I didn't know but what I did know was that I wasn't alone. Beside me was a man, a black man, with long braids. For some reason, his name I knew, his story I knew. He had torn holes in his work clothes and a frown on his face.

"He asked if I could see him and I said yes, you see he was a ghost, of a forgotten man. He had saw his family ride this train many times before but could not talk to them. Since the cops pulled him over because of a stop light and then stopped his breathing, he couldn't communicate with them ever again. He asked if I could see him and I said yes, and I wondered was I a necromancer? In front of me, a young caramel skinned man sat next to his mother.

"His Do-rag tight over his head that rested on his mother's shoulders. If he moved an inch he would fall through her, for ghost cannot touch what is alive, they phase through matter with no hesitation, with sadness that the living can't connect with them. His mother had tried to reach him before he had left for a party but a sheriff had caught him before she could say don't go out with your skin complexion, it's lethal. He tries to hug his mother but she can't feel him, she can only cry out his name.

"She's being haunted and doesn't even know it. A young kid my color, dark brown, sat two seats down with the rope around his neck that he was hung with. He had only seen seven, he had only seen cartoons, cheese and crackers for lunch and bath time at night but he didn't get to see graduation, or his wedding day, or a child being born from his seed – no, he saw death at the hands of racist. This was a ghost ship, or should I say a ghost train where all phantoms met at night to be alone together.

"I looked at the boy and said I can see you too.

You're not invisible anymore. I know you and I'll tell your story to the world. I heard a voice say if you can see them then I know you can see me.

"He twirled around on his tiptoes and spun like he had no cares. His braids in need of retouching, his tank top torn in the middle where his heart met a bullet, his smile bright, and his eyes examining his dance moves. I clapped for him because he was so good. As he went on switching his positions I wondered how long he had danced for eyes that could not see him, and tried to get applause from ears who could not hear the rhythm he moved to and like the grieving mother or the family of the man next to me I was being haunted too because he was my ghost, my personal poltergeist.

"I wanted to ask him why he danced when no one could see him. I wanted to say you're dead, just rest no one can see how good you can hold position and how well you could spin on your heel. I thought to myself how many of my black brothers were killed, murdered, slain by racist, bigots, American terrorist and haters? How many? How many killers went on not being prosecuted or given a fair trial for the lives they took?

"These men all pointed to me and told me to live for them. That's what they kept saying, and I got scared, I was being targeted now and they kept saying over and over again, live for us, live for us, live for us, and they wouldn't stop until I grabbed my ears, knelt down and said I will, I will – I promise I will. And then I awoke."

He didn't expect so much applause from an audience of mourners but was glad that he didn't have to walk away in awkward silence. Apparently, the woman that was sitting next to him, in the Dalmatian coat, was Othello's grandmother, and she introduced herself that way. She applauded for him once again, this time softer than the audience before, and pinched his cheek while thanking him.

21 FORGIVENESS

Moments later, Sapphire was ready to go and could no longer stand to look at his friend's casket any longer. He shook hands with Othello's grandmother, got up from his seat and headed down the aisle.

As he walked on trying not to turn back and look at the body of Othello, he heard someone call his name. It was Leonidas, and he was not afraid to yell out Sapphire's name no matter who was speaking at the time. With his feet moving faster than before, he walked towards the two double doors of the funeral home, hoping that he could leave before having to personally tell Leonidas to leave him alone.

As he got outside and felt the cool air burn his face he stopped. Leonidas had walked out with him; he could feel his eyes looking at him.

"You know, I didn't think your poems could be any more a–amazing than they already were, but the one you just did blew me away, brother," Leonidas said as he placed his hands in his pocket.

"I am not your brother," said Sapphire. "Now, my limo is waiting on me and I've gotta get home."

"You got a driver, a personal chauffeur?"

"Yup, all thanks to your zombie spell. At least one

of your voodoo tricks aren't making me spiral into a whirlwind of regret."

Leonidas ignored his jab, "I see you still wear that hat I got you. And it suits you best cause it really represents who you are. Most magicians that did magic shows back in the day we're really—"

"Magicians," Sapphire said, "I know, my mother told me."

Leonidas grinned, "And some of them were superiors, and they wore black hats to symbolize their great power among less talented magicians."

"I'm sorry, thanks for the magical history lesson, but I don't think you know that I don't want anything to do with you so I'm gonna just show it in my actions," Sapphire said, but as he turned to leave he was grabbed by Leonidas's, his ring-covered fingers gripping ahold of Sapphire's arm.

"Don't touch me!" Sapphire said as he pounded on Leonidas's chest. "Don't touch me!" Leonidas grabbed on to Sapphire's shoulders and pulled him in as he broke down.

"Why is all of this happening to me?!" Sapphire cried so hard in Leonidas's grasp, he could feel the voodoo King's arms around him as all the people that had hurt him thumped around in his mind. All the damage, all the drama they brought into his life.

When he pounded on Leonidas's chest he released his built up aggression but regretted hitting him as hard as he did. Still, he had love for Leonidas, but just not enough to let go of his deceitful ways. "Why, why do people have to hurt me, Leonidas?"

"Because people are human, and they make mistakes, just like you," said Leonidas. "They do horrible things to good people because they're not perfect...and sometimes they become selfish."

It felt good to cry in Leonidas' arms. Sapphire missed the compassion that he showed, along with his will to understand and listen.

"I just want to live a happy life...I just want to be happy, that's all I want," Sapphire said. "Leonidas, I could have stopped it all. All this power I have, I just stood there, I was a coward. I let him shoot Othello."

"No, no, you didn't."

"I did – "

"You did nothing wrong, brother, you did nothing wrong," Leonidas said.

"I just can't go on, I've tried to get over it." Sapphire let out all that he could.

"I know, I know," said Leonidas.

Forgiveness was a thing that Sapphire couldn't fully grasp onto like others had. He knew it was important but it just didn't seem available to him, especially not after the things he had been through.

There were six people that he needed to forgive: his father, Seraphina, Cerberus, Bartholomew, Leonidas and himself. He knew, above all, that forgiving himself for the many things he had done would be most difficult. Just the look of fear that Bartholomew's children had kept him in a shiver, but taking their father made his heart freeze over.

"I've got to, I've got to go," said Sapphire as he slipped out of Leonidas' grip. He walked down his steps as Leonidas stood with his hands now in his pockets again.

"I'll always love you, my brother," said Leonidas as he watched Sapphire open the door of the limousine. "I'll always love you. You might hate me, but I have found love in you, and inspiration and joy and for that, I'll cherish you, always. You will have a home at Boon Hood until the day that I die."

That stopped Sapphire from getting in. Thinking of Leonidas' death, his future head injury, made Sapphire turn around. This might be the last time, he thought, say it back.

"I...I'll always love you too, Leonidas," Sapphire said. "Really...."

"Do you forgive me?" Leonidas asked, his afro blowing in the winds gust.

Sapphire didn't respond. He turned around and got into the limousine as he held onto the top of his black fedora. "Goodbye Leonidas," he said.

He felt horrible, his eyes now a glossy red. How could he look at Leonidas in such a humble state and still not offer him forgiveness? Sapphire questioned himself as he told the driver to drive on, not providing a destination. He asked himself how he could be so mean to the man that had taken him in and fed him without charge, paid him to teach magic and listened to his problems.

Sapphire was furious, at everything and at everyone.

He hated murder, he hated deceit, he even loathed Othello's mother for allowing such a foul man into her son's life. He was disgusted with the driver that refused to let Othello ride and he despised every policeman that had taken the life of an innocent man.

"Just take me around town or something. Patrol around."

He needed to ride. Moving around made him think, he could take in New York's fine architecture and analyze his thoughts more clearly while in a car.

It was getting dark out, and Sapphire noticed that he was slowly creeping into the ghetto.

He looked out of his window and saw what appeared to be a prostitute in shabby clothing leaning into a green station wagon window. He hated that too, women selling their bodies.

Being surrounded by his grandmother, aunt and mother's radiating confidence and dignity made him loathe when women gave themselves away for currency. Two black men, in thick coats and wheat colored boots, smoked as they leaned against the wall and eyed the black limousine that turned on their corner. Three young black boys were in his eye view and they awed as he passed them up. They leaned down and took in the view of someone that looked like them and was young like them traveling in an exquisite ride.

He looked over at his right side and saw a policeman shoving yet another black man against a brick wall as blue and red lights painted an alerting flash on the scene.

"First they paint our streets red and blue," whispered Sapphire as he looked at the zombie-fied driver through the review mirror. "Then they paint our body's red and our family's blue."

He placed his face in his hands as he sobbed, remembering how it all happened. The loud bang, the bloodshed, the evil in Bartholomew's eyes.

Why did innocent people have to die? Why was racism still even flourishing after all the marches and love labor? Who did Bartholomew think he was to take a mother's son?

Sapphire looked over at Othello's obituary and placed his wet hand that was covered in sweat and tears over its surface.

Who could take out this pain in him? Who could save him from losing his mind or taking his own life? He didn't want to live anymore with his guilt or without his friend.

He thought of Pastor Ruby and his words. People had said that God could heal any wound and mend every broken heart, but that was all just opinion to him.

God was a part of Crystal and Topaz's life; they prayed to him and even asked for forgiveness. God seemed to bring them peace and he wondered if he could have that same peace.

Crystal had hurt and had been hurt before, just like him, he was sure of it. He wondered if the same God that heard the prayers of his church ruled over Pastor Ruby's as well.

He gave the driver a few directions, seeing that he was close to Joy in the Word Non-denominational church. With huffing and puffing, Sapphire tried to get himself together as he gathered his strength.

The driver pulled up to the small church and Sapphire walked out to the front, stepping on the wet ground that was sprinkled by drizzling rain.

He eyed the driver, who looked clueless and said, "Go, drive back to your station. I release you from my spell, be free, go!"

The driver blinked and blinked until he was back to his normal mind, his eyes no longer white. Sapphire walked towards the church as the limousine driver drove off, without asking any questions, fulfilling Sapphire's last commandment to be released.

He gripped the wet, brass handle of the wooden door and opened it. Something was drawing him here, something inside needed to come and see if God could heal him.

Inside was a small church smaller than Crystal's Catholic church. He could smell the scent of sugar cookies and took in the lights that were strung around a tree in the corner.

Two women with little children, a man on a rickety organ and Pastor Ruby himself looked at Sapphire as he walked in with hesitation, while he silently sobbed.

Pastor Ruby, in a bright red suit, hopped from behind his pulpit and approached Sapphire as he slowly moved his feet.

All he kept hearing was that he needed to be forgiven so that he could be happy again. But he couldn't forgive himself so someone else had to do it.

Someone that was rumored to be all powerful. Sapphire learned that he had power and that it was great, but had learned that he was not all mighty or all powerful.

Everyone's face became full of concern as he sniffled and shivered while walking closer to Pastor Ruby. "I need forgiveness, for all I have done, for everything I have done to others and to myself. I need help, because I don't wanna continue to live without happiness."

Pastor Ruby stood in front of Sapphire as he grabbed his shoulders. "Son, you need to be saved before you can be truly happy. Do you want to accept Jesus into your heart, because he can give you happiness, he can restore your joy, do you?"

"Yes, whatever it takes," said Sapphire. "Whatever it takes."

"Well, repeat after me, father I have sinned

against you and I confess with my mouth that I have."

Sapphire repeated his words.

"Good, good," said Pastor Ruby. "Now, say Lord I believe that you rose from the dead and I now ask that you come into my life and make me a new creature."

Sapphire, with his eyes, shut tight, repeated his words, yet again, as everyone around stood up to witness what was taking place.

Pastor Ruby gripped tighter on Sapphire's shoulder, "now you are saved. And know this son, that when you stand praying, forgive others that have trespassed against you so that God will forgive you of all the trespassing, all the sin, all the hurt that you have caused him as well, and he will forgive you. Do you forgive everyone that has hurt you, do you?"

Pastor Ruby spoke with such a thundering voice as the compassion of the gospel flamed in his eyes.

To him, love represented forgiveness.

Sapphire bellowed out, "I forgive them all, every last single person that ever hurt me, I forgive…I forgive them."

He lost control of his legs and fell, but not on the ground; but into the arms of Pastor Ruby, who ushered him down with love and with care.

All that he could say was that he had forgiven everyone. Over and over again.

A Lost Chapter from Jay Hunter's first novel. Titled: A Black Girl Named Bambi.

Enjoy

On The Road

Tiny and Bambi held hands most of the drive towards Arkansas. With determination and strength, the two pressed on to a new life. A fresh start. They didn't know where they would find work but Tiny assured that he'd find something fast.

They drove through all sorts of towns stopping for pictures along the way.

They stopped to see the world's largest hair pick in Biloxi Mississippi and ate lunch at a restaurant outside of town where people talked much faster than Bambi did. She could barely understand them

"We gone be alright, baby," Tiny would say, whenever Bambi would hide her face in her hands. Memories of her old life appeared in her head. Her house, and its deformed body burning from smoldering heat – and those boy's, they did all this.

Tiny couldn't have his girl thinking on her past too long so he'd do little things such as pinching her cheek when she'd get too quiet or singing her a song when she'd shed a tear.

With just an hour left on the drive to Daddy Author's, Tiny stopped Bambi at a 24 seven diner for breakfast and then they would rest in the car afterward.

They really turned a 7-hour drive into a 28-hour one because of shopping, resting and touring around foreign towns.

Bambi had stepped out of the car in

new pumps a black leather jacket and a long flowery summer dress, all gifts from her man.

Tiny had a blue collar shirt he had bought from a gas station rack and slacks. His hair was starting to grow into a small afro.

"Good Lord, It's time to cut this hair again," he said as he looked at his image in is car window.

"I think you look fine, baby," Bambi said as she picked at Tiny's hair.

The two sat at the bar and listened to jokes from the cook as they waited on their food. Like always, she watched him scarf down as much as he could while she tried to eat ladylike, just as her grandmother taught. But that flew out the window when the waitress who had a tall afro in a blue scarf brought out seconds of hot French toast.

"Keep 'em coming!" Bambi said as she fanned at her food.

"Girl, you love you some French toast, huh?" Tiny asked as the waitress placed both her hands on his shoulders.

What is she doing? Bambi thought as she squinted at the waitress.

"Watch your hands there, Miss Lady," said Tiny as he took her hands from off his shoulders. He wasn't stupid, he saw Bambi's eyes.

"I'm sorry, I'm sorry," the waitress said as she popped her gum, her red lipstick glistening in the lights above. "You can call me, Bernice, sweetheart. Bernice Wellington."

She winked at Tiny hard enough to cause her fake lashes to fall off.

"Well, Bernice, can you get me some more orange juice," Bambi asked, her eyes still squinted.

Bernice rolled her eyes, "it ain't even empty yet, suga',"

"I'm not yo' suga'," Bambi said.

"Hey, hey," said Tiny as he grabbed Bambi's wrist. "Hey, Miss Bernice, can you please grab my wife another orange juice. I sho' would appreciate it."

Wife? Did he call her his wife? She

almost kissed him then. He was really trying to be boyfriend of the year, she thought. Her Tiny always knew how to turn a situation around.

"Okay, honey," said Bernice as she winked at Tiny before walking away; her hips switching from east and west.

"Wife?" Bambi breathed as Tiny grinned. "I'm yo' wife – was that a proposal?"

"I don't know, maybe, no, I don't know," said Tiny as he held Bambi's hands. "Maybe...if you'll say yes."

Bambi's stomach jolted. "Well, if you ever asked, of course –"

"Here you go, honey," said Bernice as she plopped an orange juice on the bar in front of Bambi.

That was quick, Bambi thought.

Then, she leaned her way in between the two, facing Tiny with a wide smile.

"So, what y'all doing down in Arkansas? Y'all from here?" she asked.

"What – excuse me, Bernice, we was talking?" said Tiny.

Bernice shifted back in her position. "Sorry, again, I'm sorry. I just love seeing young love (Bambi rolled her eyes) it's rare. How long y'all been together?"

Bernice asked her question politely but only faced Tiny as she leaned her butt against Bambi's leg.

This was the last straw.

Bernice's eyes were on Tiny like she was a predator. "You know, these young girls are sweet and all, but they can't cook you a hot meal, run ya' water and raise your chillin' like a grown woman can? You know what I mean?"

Bambi parted her lips and whispered an incantation, "Ojuno," silently enough for Tiny not to hear.

"Oh – wow, yeah, I know what you mean?" Tiny said as he glared at Bernice who's eyes had crossed.

"I mean, I ain't trying to be rude, honey, I know you happy and all but are you really satisfied," Bernice said her eyes, making Tiny wanna split at the

8

seams.

Bambi had learned very mischievous spells from her Uncle Charlie who had a book of Nigerian jinx's written in Yoruba, an African tongue.

"Can I have some more sausage links?" asked Tiny as he placed his fist over his mouth.

"Sure, anything for my hungry guy."

Bambi eyed the waitress as she walked away and said, "Buburo Iruno."

Bernice walked past Tiny and swayed while her proud afro vanished from her scalp.

"Stop," said Tiny as he grabbed a hold of Bambi's hands. "I know that's you, stop, with yo' fast self."

"Not done yet," Bambi said.

"Yes, you are, yes, stop, Jenevieve."

Bambi laughed. "Don't call me by my first name, Virgil, you not my Daddy.

"I am tonight," said Tiny.

Before Bernice could go fetch Tiny's order, she visited another table that couldn't help but smile wide when her crossed eyes approached them.

"Bernice what done happened to you, girl?" asked the cook, stopping her from entering the back of the diner.

"What do you mean, Rufus?" Bernice asked as she turned to look at her reflection in a mirror above a record player.

Tiny slapped his money on the table and grabbed Bambi as Bernice screamed her head off.

"What happened to my eyes? My hair?"

"It'll grow back, heffa'," said Bambi as Tiny placed his hand over her mouth.

"Well, y'all have a good night," he said as he ushered Bambi outside. "The food was mighty nice."

<u>ABOUT THE AUTHOR</u>

Jay Hunter is an African American renaissance man. He grew up in the arts with two artistic parents, who helped sculpt his career as a writer, singer, and musician. He currently lives in Missouri where he enjoys creating, writing, music, his family and his artistic community. He chose himself for the cover of this book because he was the9 spitting image of Sapphire Silas Bell.

www.ingramcontent.com/pod-product-compliance
Lightning Source LLC
Chambersburg PA
CBHW021421170526
45164CB00001B/37